"This sobering book meticulously documents the teachings of Islam on women and marriage from both the Qur'an and a wide range of Islamic sources. As a woman I found it devastating and chilling to read the 'rationale' behind the marginalization, use, and abuse of women for centuries. However, this book does not leave us in a place of hopelessness, but instead offers a radically different way of viewing marriage, men, and women—the teachings of Jesus Christ. This book is a must read for Muslim and Christian women alike and for anyone seeking a deeper understanding of current events and the plight of women in the world today." —**Marta Rusten MacDougall, Clinical Psychologist**

"How fitting a title for this book! Truly my heart was heavy as I was reminded again of the bondage and burdens placed upon women by unbiblical teachings but then rejoiced to read of the hope that they have in God's word. Dr. Zaka and Mrs. Coleman have presented clearly and concisely the differences between man's view of women and God's view of women. May God use this book to bring many women into a personal relationship with Jesus Christ and to give them a great anticipation of meeting the perfect bridegroom who will love them eternally." —**Evelyn Wallace, Former WIC President and Muslim Women's Speaker**

"Zaka and Coleman do a superb job of clarifying the issues women face between a Biblical and an Islamic worldview. Going to the original sources from both traditions, the reader will find the contrasts striking and the outcome in life going from slavery to freedom. A must-read for every Christian woman who relates to Muslims and every Muslim woman who is open to what is available outside her tradition." —**Bruce McDowell, Minister of Missions, Tenth Presbyterian Church**

"I was reading through this book the first time while waiting for medical tests with my daughter. When we were called into the room, a woman wearing a Muslim headscarf greeted me. I immediately told her I was reading this book, and we talked quite easily for about twenty minutes. I came away from the room so saddened by her plight, so sad to think of what she did not know about Jesus and the life He has for His daughters. Years ago I would never have begun a conversation, but the authors have taught me so much, and through this book the Lord has given me a desire to reach out to Muslim women." —**Barbara Lerch, Editor, P&R Publishing**

"Coming out of Islam and understanding these colorful cages that Muslim women have been put into just breaks my heart. For that reason, *Cry of the Heart and Quest of the Mind* is a wonderful resource, which I highly recommend to my sisters in Islam around the world to read and reflect on carefully, with the prayer that they would experience the freedom that Jesus has given me." —**Maher Salhani, AMF and CWW Missionary**

"We African-American women and men strongly recommend *Cry of the Heart and Quest of the Mind* to our dear sisters who have become Muslims. Read it carefully with an open mind and loving heart to find out what you have in the Noble Qur'an and what Christ of the Holy Bible has done for you on the Cross. We pray for you who will read this book: that you will meet Jesus Christ who restored your dignity and honor and that you will be touched by His redeeming love and become His bride for eternity." —**Chandra D. Jones, Dea Elayne J. Johnson, Betty Patterson, Jefferson Young Jr., Annette Lamkin, Deacon John Johnson, Pastor Wilbert S. Richardson, Students at Biblical Institute for Islamic Studies, Philadelphia**

"Reading this book was a startling eye-opener to the realities of the plight of women in the Muslim world. In some ways the American media has not given us a clear picture of the practices of Islam, leading us to believe the real message of Islam is love, kindness, and peace for all people. After reading *Cry of the Heart and Quest of the Mind*, I realize the seemingly 'Christian attitudes' that are being propagated about Islam are dangerously untrue, especially for women, and now understand that it is a perverseness that must be truthfully revealed and overcome through the power of Christ. I rejoiced as I read the many Scripture verses in chapter 7 that free women from their oppressive bondage and give them hope for the future. Hope is found only in Jesus Christ, and this book presents that hope and a better life for women of Islam." —**Betty F. Hasiuk, Teacher and Church Music Director**

"My heart was overwhelmed by the comparisons between Muslim women and Christian women. As Christians we have been drenched in the love of our Lord Jesus Christ and our place as God's children, men and women together. As an adult leader of girls I have made it my responsibility to show them how we were made in God's image, to love one another, serve one another out of that love, and to find ourselves as valuable in God's eyes. The message to Islamic women is so contrary to that image that we need to cry out to them, and this book lovingly does so." —**Kathleen Bender, Calvary Presbyterian Church Office Manager, Girl Scout Leader, Former President Immanuel Lutheran Church Council**

"Having grown up in a Middle Eastern home in America, and having studied Islam on the undergraduate and graduate level, I highly recommend *Cry of the Heart and Quest of the Mind* as an in-depth volume for the study and understanding of Muslim and Christian

women's search for religious truth and honor. Because of my many years of experience working with Church Without Walls, I would be very comfortable using this book as an extension of friendship, witness, and inquiry to my Muslim colleagues with the goal of leading them to discover the liberating grace of Jesus Christ for humanity."
—Alfred Siha, Writing Tutor, Penn State University

"Your book is a must-read for Christian women to be able to minister effectively to Muslim women! I was reminded again that Christians need to be on their knees in prayer for these women, not only for their physical and mental protection, but that the truth of the gospel of Christ will penetrate the teaching that surrounds them in every aspect of their lives. Oh that every Muslim woman could see the truth and freedom that can only be found in Jesus Christ! As a homeschooling mom, this book will be a great addition to my world history and world religion curriculums." **—Lisa Supplee, WIC President, Eastern PA Presbytery (PCA)**

Cry of the Heart
— *and* —
Quest of the Mind

Cry of the Heart
— and —
Quest of the Mind

An Analysis of Muslim and Christian
Women's Search for Truth and Honor

Anees Zaka & Diane Coleman

"Seeking Better Understanding"
Church Without Walls
PRESBYTERIAN CHURCH IN AMERICA
PHILADELPHIA, PA

© 2006 by Church Without Walls

All rights reserved. No part of this book shall be reproduced or transmitted in any form or by any means, electronic, mechanical, magnetic, photographic including photocopying, recording, or any information storage and retrieval system, without prior written permission of the publisher, Church Without Walls, P.O. Box 27276, Philadelphia, PA 19118. No patent liability is assumed with respect to the use of the information contained herein. Although every precaution has been taken in the preparation of this book, the publisher and authors assume no responsibility for errors or omissions. Neither is any liability assumed for damages resulting from the use of the information contained herein.

Unless otherwise indicated, Scripture quotations are from The Holy Bible, English Standard Version, copyright © 2001 by Crossway Bibles, a division of Good News Publishers. Used by permission. All rights reserved.

Emphasis within Scripture quotations have been added.

Qur'an quotations are from Abdullah Yusuf Ali, *The Qur'an: Text, Translation, and Commentary*, U.S. Edition, 2001.

Emphasis within Qur'an quotations have been added.

[other credits]

Page design by Tobias Design

Typesetting by Lakeside Design Plus

Printed in the United States of America

ISBN 10: 0-9786312-0-X

ISBN 13: 978-09786312-0-X

Library of Congress Control Number: 2006932554

To

Our Lord Jesus Christ who liberated women from their bondage and restored their dignity once and for all by giving His life for them. And as a result of His unconditional love, believing women in Him became redeemed.

All of our Muslim sisters around the globe through God's creation with our deep believing prayers that someday some of you will become our sisters through Christ's redeeming grace.

All the young women in the West who have made a lifelong commitment of marriage to a Muslim man who *appears* to be the man of their dreams.

Mother Nancy J. Moffitt and her family for their prayers and support for advancing the work of the gospel among the nations.

The loving memory of Helen Harris—a wife, mother, and grandmother who planted God's redeeming love among all people.

All godly Christian women who reach out to Muslim women around the world with the love of Christ.

Contents

List of Tables xiii
Foreword xv
Preface xix

1. Creation in the Noble Qur'an 1
   The Qur'anic and Biblical creation accounts differ substantially—in the location of the garden of Eden, in what transpired there, and in the consequences of these events. If both books were given by God, why do they not agree?

2. Creation and the Fall in the Holy Bible 15
   The Bible teaches about the creation and rebellion of Satan and humanity. What was the result of the fall for manhood and womanhood?

3. Men and Women in the Noble Qur'an 35
   According to the Qur'an, men and women differ in many aspects—they are not equal in their status and human rights. What does the Qur'an teach about marriage, divorce, and domestic life?

4. Women in the Hadith 45
   The traditions concerning Muhammad's dealings with women have a major impact on their role in society today. Are women accorded the same human rights and freedoms applied to men?

5. Men and Women in Biblical Christianity 57
   Biblical teachings regarding manhood and womanhood have helped mold and establish Western civilization. Are these ideals outmoded, or are they applicable for men and women today?

6. Is Islam the Answer? 83
   Orthodox Islam has plainly-drawn laws concerning gender relationships. Does this strict code of conduct protect and benefit women?

7. A Quest of the Mind and a Cry of the Heart   103
The Christian gospel promises love, joy, and peace in the lives of those who respond. Is Islam also able to meet the needs and deepest desires of fallen men and women?

Appendix   119
Notes   123
Internet Resources   135
Scripture Index   151
Qur'an Index   155

List of Tables

Table 1: Marriage in the Noble Qur'an 36

Table 2: Women in the Noble Qur'an 41

Table 3: Hadith Regarding Muhammad's Wives 45

Table 4: Hadith Regarding Women under Islam 48

Table 5: Marriage in the Old Testament 59

Table 6: Jesus and Women in the Gospels 64

Table 7: More Women in the New Testament 69

Table 8: Marriage among Believers 73

Table 9: Jesus' Love in the New Testament 104

Table 10: Joy in the Holy Bible 108

Table 11: Peace in the Holy Bible 111

Foreword

Many centuries ago (twenty to be exact) female babies were considered a liability. During the first century, in certain parts of the world, demographics were stunningly imbalanced male to female. Female infanticide was not uncommon. Baby girls, often considered the equivalent of deformed, were killed by exposure. It was permitted by law to leave them on the dung heaps outside the city to die. As we travel through the centuries in various parts of the world, we can find many other anti-female practices, such as genital mutilation, sati (the Indian practice in which a widow, on her husband's death, would burn herself on his funeral pyre), rape as a weapon of war, and the sex trafficking of the present time. To travel in Arab countries today is to find many customs that are demeaning to women. Some, such as genital mutilation or sanctioned physical abuse, are violent and shocking to the Western mind. Other practices, such as veiling and seclusion or allowing no voice in public affairs, seem less violent, but are terribly restrictive and prevent women from full participation in their worlds.

Anees Zaka and Diane Coleman have written a book exposing both the mindsets and customs demeaning to women in the Islamic world. They have written with hearts of love for the women who are so denigrated, clearly longing to see them set free to live the full-orbed lives the God of the Old and New Testaments has intended for them. As a psychologist who has worked with many battered and abused women in the United States, it was fascinating to read many of the positions stated in the Qur'an regarding women. The teachings that women are subordinate, must provide sex for a husband on demand, are examined both physically and psychologically for their fitness for marriage, carry the responsibility for men's wrong behaviors, and are basically seen as property all suggest attitudes that are found in Western men who are abusive to women. Men have the power, the right, and the say.

Women are to provide what is required and/or desired. If they do not, they are punished. This is certainly not to suggest that all Muslim men are abusive of their wives or other women. However, whenever there is a significant imbalance of power, the risk and the likelihood of abuse increase greatly. And sadly, there have been many reports both from the media and from Islamic women themselves of battering, killing women in the name of honor, female genital mutilation, and public humiliation. Taking a stance against such attitudes toward women is dangerous, as is evidenced in the jailing of Ali Mohaqeq Nasab. Believing the promise of a free press in Afghanistan, Nasab printed essays in his monthly magazine, *Women's Rights*, questioning legal discrimination against women. He had the audacity to suggest that a woman's testimony in court should be given the same weight as a man's, rather than half. As a result, he was sentenced to two years in prison and two hundred religious scholars and clerics have issued a fatwa that he should be given three days to repent or be hanged.

Even a cursory study of the life and ministry of Jesus Christ when he was here in the flesh reveals one who never denigrated women, never blamed them for the sins of men, did not cast them away as dangerous, nor treated them as unimportant. Instead, we see God in the flesh gracing the womb of a virgin, being blessed by a prophetess in the temple, blessing a bride of Cana, and raising a widow's son from the dead. We also see this God raising women to the position of honored student, as fellow companions on the way and tellers of the gospel story. He offered dignity, safety, and honor to the women who populated his life. In reading this book, it becomes very clear that it is the heartfelt desire of Anees Zaka and Diane Coleman to offer those same gifts to the women of Islam through the life and love of our Lord Jesus Christ. With them, my heart longs to see all women of this world who find themselves in some kind of manmade bondage set free by the great King and Lover of their souls. May this book contribute to that end.

    Diane Langberg, Ph.D.
    Psychologist

Preface

This book is a sequel to our first book, *The Truth about Islam.* Both books are unique since they were written through the professional collaboration of a man and a woman, each born into very different cultures—yet united in spirit through Christ Jesus. Each was deeply impressed by the "quest of the mind" and clearly heard the "cry of the heart" of our Muslim sisters in God's creation around the globe.

We wrote this book with open minds and loving hearts. In our desire to be fair and "speak the truth in love," we went to the original sources—the Noble Qur'an and the Holy Bible—to bring the texts that speak on this issue to light. Therefore, the reader is strongly encouraged to reflect on both texts in order to fully understand what they say.

We spent nearly two years researching this topic from various angles and sources. We also set aside time for prayer and fasting to ask God to lead us by His Holy Spirit to write accurately. We hope it serves three useful purposes:

First, to provide information to women who live under Qur'anic Islam and who are not fully aware of the true teachings of the Noble Qur'an and the Hadith regarding them and their issues.

Second, to fully inform Western women who are dating Muslim men of what they will experience should they enter into marriage.

Third, to instruct all women who desire to know the true teachings of the Noble Qur'an and the Holy Bible concerning manhood and womanhood.

Our main goal in this book is not to show the superiority of the Biblical view of women. Rather, it is to show the status of women under Islam as presented in the Noble Qur'an and the Hadith. We hope that our readers will see and be touched by our love and concern for them—free of unfounded criticism and insensitivity.

Our believing prayer to our Lord Jesus Christ is that some of our Muslim sisters who read this book will see the light of the gospel and will be led by the Holy Spirit to surrender their lives to Him Who alone is able to give them new life and restore their dignity. If this happens to only one dear woman, then we will consider our efforts rewarded and not in vain.

May that day come soon and become a reality in the lives of millions of Muslim women.

Anees Zaka

Creation in the Noble Qur'an

From the very beginning, God assigned to His creatures maleness and femaleness. Therefore, gender is God's idea—and it is a perfectly wonderful idea!

In order to trace the development of the relationship between men and women throughout history, we must start at the very beginning—when God created the first human pair. What do Islamic theologians believe and teach? And does their teaching agree with the Biblical account?

The creation sections of the Noble Qur'an are interspersed throughout its text. Sura 2:30–39 is the longest, most coherent narrative. Perhaps the most respected English edition of the Qur'an is the translation by Yusuf Ali, with both text and notes.

Sura 2:30–39

> 30. Behold, thy Lord said to the angels: "I will create a *vicegerent* on earth." They said: "Wilt Thou place therein one who *will make mischief* therein and *shed blood*?—Whilst we

do celebrate Thy praises and glorify Thy holy (name)?" He said: "I know what ye know not."

31. And He taught Adam the nature of all things; then He placed them before the angels, and said: "Tell Me the nature of these if ye are right."

32. They said: "Glory to Thee: Of knowledge we have none, save what Thou hast taught us: In truth it is Thou who art perfect in knowledge and wisdom."

33. He said: "O Adam! Tell them their natures." When he had told them, Allah said: "Did I not tell you that I know the secrets of heaven and earth, and I know what ye reveal and what ye conceal?"

34. And behold, *We said to the angels: "Bow down to Adam:" And they bowed down: Not so Iblis: He refused and was haughty: He was of those who reject Faith.*

35. We said: "O Adam! Dwell thou and thy wife in the Garden; and eat of the bountiful things therein as (where and when) ye will; but approach not this tree, or ye run into harm and transgression."

36. Then did Satan make them slip from the (Garden), and get them out of the state (of felicity) in which they had been. We said: "*Get ye down*, all (ye people) with enmity between yourselves. *On earth will be your dwelling place* and your means of livelihood—for a time."

37. Then learnt Adam from his Lord words of inspiration, and his Lord turned towards him, for He is Oft-Returning, Most Merciful.

38. We said: "Get ye down all from here; and if, as is sure, there comes to you guidance from Me, whosoever follows My guidance, on them shall be no fear, nor shall they grieve."

39. "But those who reject Faith and belie Our Signs, they shall be Companions of the Fire; they shall abide therein."

DIFFERENCES BETWEEN THE CREATION ACCOUNTS IN THE NOBLE QUR'AN AND HOLY BIBLE

In the Qur'anic account, the two categories of separately created beings witness the creation of man: angels and jinn. Allah created both jinn and angels from a substance described as "fire." The word "jinn" is the origin of our English word "genie."

There are no fallen angels in Islam,[1] therefore Iblis must be categorized as a jinn. But the doctrine of fallen angels is attested to in the Holy Bible in Isaiah 14:12–15, Jude 6, and Matthew 25:41.

In Islamic theology, jinn are unseen spirits that roam about the earth, serving Allah by causing mischief for mankind. Iblis, or Satan, the only being of this kind specifically named, is accursed because he refused to bow down to Adam. The focus is on man as God's "strongman" on earth, deserving of worship by all of Allah's creation. Iblis's refusal classifies him among "those who reject Faith [Islam]." This is the meaning of the term "infidel."

Man is *never* to be worshipped in the Holy Bible. Only Yahweh is deserving of worship. (In fact, one of the proofs of the divinity of Jesus Christ is that He accepts the worship of men and women, which is always reserved exclusively for God.) It is interesting that the Noble Qur'an switches to the use of the pronoun "him" instead of "them" when prescribing angelic obeisance, implying that only the Islamic man, not the woman, is to receive the worship and honor of angelic beings.

Islamic angels differ from mankind in that they have no emotions. According to Islamic thought, mankind is unique in that it has been given the gift of emotion as a companion to the power of will so he could "steer his own bark."[2]

None of this information appears in the Holy Bible. Although a thorough discussion of the Biblical doctrine of angels is beyond the scope of this book, it should be noted that the Holy Bible confirms that angels have emotions. They sing in joyful praise (see Psalms 103:20; 148:2; Luke 2:13–15; 15:10). They "long" to understand and participate in the salvation given to men (see 1 Peter 1:12). The archangel Michael "contended" with the devil and rebuked him (see Jude 9). All of these passages demonstrate emotional responses.

In the Noble Qur'an, the angels counsel Allah, warning him that man will be a mischief-maker and killer. Nowhere in the Holy Bible do angelic beings ever "counsel" the Biblical God, Yahweh. In Biblical theology, angels are God's messengers, worshippers, and ministers. They constitute His heavenly army, carry out His commands, and are present in the heavenly court. But they are never His advisors.

According to the Noble Qur'an, males are given "more" of something, which gives them the power to be protectors and maintainers of women and to have authority over them. It is uncertain what this "something" actually is. Yusuf Ali added the word "strength" parenthetically in his interpretation of the text. However, according to Islamic Hadith, "more" has been interpreted to include many other qualities, attributes, and endowments, giving Muslim men superior status and control over women. Chapter 6 will address this in more detail.

The Qur'anic Garden Was Not on Earth

Islam teaches that the garden of Eden was a heavenly "spiritual existence." When Allah told man to "go down," He was relegating him to a lower place, which is the earth. The Islamic garden is described as having no enmity or evil.[3] Additionally, man is said to be gradually tempted from his "higher" to "lower" state.[4] Yet this is confusing, since Iblis is taught to have been specifically placed there by Allah for the purpose of tempting mankind (Sura 7:22). Thus, evil was introduced into the Qur'anic garden by Allah himself, and therefore it could not have been a place without enmity, as Ali describes and Islamic theology teaches.

Both Jews and Biblical Christians affirm that the garden of Eden was located on earth, probably in present-day Iraq. Its geographical location is described in Genesis 2:8–15.

The use of the plural "We" for Allah is explained as a plural of "respect and honor" and used for "royal proclamations."[5] This explanation is also used as a Christian apologetic for Yahweh's use of plurality in the Genesis creation narrative. But historically, Biblical Christian theologians have seen the plural as a reference to the complex unity of the Godhead, more specifically, the tri-unity of God (see Appendix).

Ali explains that when Allah wishes to denote a "special personal relationship, he uses the singular." His comment regarding a "special personal relationship" between man and Allah is a direct contradiction of mainstream Islamic doctrine. Islam takes great pains not to describe Allah with any identifiable attributes or characteristics at all. The fact that Allah has no personality effectively eliminates any possibility of a personal relationship between Him and humanity.[6]

Thus, the creation accounts of the Holy Bible and Noble Qur'an present two very different gardens, different human prototypes, and different purposes and outcomes. The popular and dangerously misleading notion that the information in the Noble Qur'an supplements, corrects, or builds upon the Biblical account is clearly refuted. These are two very different concepts of creation, reflecting two very separate realizations of God.

In light of these evidences, the Noble Qur'an and Holy Bible are totally different books. They did not come from the same God.

The Seduction of Man
Sura 20:115–124

115. We had already, beforehand, taken the covenant of Adam but *he forgot*: And We found, on his part, no firm resolve.

116. When We said to the angels, "Prostrate yourselves to Adam", they prostrated themselves, but not Iblis: He refused.

117. Then We said: "O Adam! Verily, this is an enemy to thee and thy wife: So let him not get you both out of the Garden so that thou art landed in misery.

118. "There is therein (enough provision) for thee not to go hungry *nor to go naked,*

119. "Nor to suffer from thirst, nor from the sun's heat."

120. But Satan whispered evil to him: He said, "O Adam! Shall I lead thee to the *Tree of Eternity* and to *a kingdom* that never decays?"

121. In the result, they both ate of the tree, and so their nakedness appeared to them: They began to sew together, for their covering, leaves from the Garden: Thus did Adam disobey his Lord, and *allow himself to be seduced.*

122. But his Lord chose him (for His Grace): He turned to him and gave him guidance.

123. He said: "Get ye down, both of you,—all together, from the Garden, with enmity one to another: But if, as is sure, there comes to you guidance from Me, whosoever follows My guidance, will not lose his way, nor fall into misery.

124. "But whosoever turns away from My Message, verily for him is *a life narrowed down*, and We shall raise him up blind on the Day of Judgment."

Sura 7:19–27

19. "O Adam! Dwell thou and thy wife in the Garden, and enjoy (its good things) as ye wish: But approach not this tree, or ye run into harm and transgression."

20. Then began Satan to whisper suggestions to them, bringing openly before their minds *all their shame that was hidden from them* (before): He said: "Your Lord only forbade you this tree, lest ye should become angels or such beings as live forever."

21. And he swore to them both, that he was their sincere adviser.

22. So by deceit he brought about their fall: When they tasted of the tree, their *shame became manifest* to them, and they began to sew together the leaves of the Garden over their bodies. And their Lord called unto them: "Did I not forbid you that tree, and *tell you that Satan was an avowed enemy unto you?*"

23. They said: "Our Lord! We have *wronged our own souls*: If Thou forgive us not and bestow not upon us Thy Mercy, we shall certainly be lost."

24. (Allah) said: "Get ye down, with enmity between yourselves. *On earth will be your dwelling place* and your means of livelihood,—for a time."

25. He said: "Therein shall ye live, and therein shall ye die; but from it shall ye be taken out (at last)."

26. O ye Children of Adam! We have *bestowed raiment upon you* to cover your shame, as well as to be an adornment to you. But the *raiment of righteousness,*—that is the best. Such are among the Signs of Allah, that they may receive admonition!

27. O ye Children of Adam! *Let not Satan seduce you*, in the same manner as he got your parents out of the Garden, *stripping them of their raiment*, to expose their shame: For *he and his tribe* watch you from a position where ye cannot see them: We made the Evil Ones friends (only) to those without Faith.

THE BASICS OF ISLAMIC DOCTRINE

Embedded within these passages are some very essential doctrines critical to understanding the relationship between men and women in Islam.

Newly-created man and woman, according to Islam, were from the very beginning extremely forgetful and lacked resolve or commitment to the law of Allah.[7] Humanity's fundamental problem is his *inability to remember and perform* according to God's commands. This is just a simple "failing," not a tragic flaw. If people are constantly and consistently reminded, all will be well. Thus, the primary task and purpose of the Noble Qur'an, shari'ah law, and all Islamic civil and religious authority is to remind Muslims continually of their many obligations before Allah. Legal procedures and social pressures ensure obedience. Threats and public punishment make examples of offenders.

Allah placed Satan in the garden for the specific purpose of being an adversary to mankind, introducing disharmony and enmity into the Qur'anic garden. The tree forbidden to Adam and his wife in the Noble Qur'an is the Tree of *Eternity*, not the Biblical Tree of the Knowledge of Good and Evil. Satan's tactic in the Islamic version was to appeal to man's lust and hunger for *personal power ("a kingdom") and divine immortality ("never decays")*.[8] In the Biblical account, Eve's desire for wisdom (to be "like God, knowing good and evil") is what brings about their disobedience. Chapter 2 will explore these ideas more thoroughly. But for now, it is important to realize that the Qur'anic temptation is fundamentally different from that described in Biblical Christianity.

Humanity Must "Make Good"

The original man and woman, according to Islam, were given "limited faculty of choice,"[9] and charged with the "training of their own will."[10] Every Muslim man and woman is born in this state and given this charge. They must get back to a state of blessedness by their own efforts. Biblical Christianity, on the other hand, teaches that this is impossible without God's intervention.

It is curious that Allah gives man the means to provide clothing for himself *before* the fall, implying that physical nakedness must not have been acceptable in the Islamic version of the garden.[11] In addition, there is a cryptic reference to a "raiment of righteousness" (Sura 7:26), implying a spiritual condition.

If the original man was clothed in a "raiment of honor" and innocence,[12] had this not come from the hand of God? And if a raiment of righteousness is to be obtained, must it not also come from the hand of God? Biblical Christianity proclaims that it must, but Islam maintains that men and women must weave this raiment themselves, from their own "virtues."[13]

In the Bible, God regarded the simple physical garment that fallen man and woman wove from the leaves of the garden as insufficient to cover the nakedness of their physical bodies. How much less sufficient must their efforts be to weave a "raiment of righteousness" to cover their spiritual selves? God Himself prepared the perfect garments of skin to cover their physical bodies after the Fall. Will not God also prepare the garment of righteousness in which their souls will be spiritually clothed? Again, this is what Biblical Christianity teaches.

The source of righteousness is a fundamental and crucial difference between Qur'anic Islam and Biblical Christianity in their views of salvation. According to Biblical Christianity, men's and women's flawed efforts to create their own garments of righteousness, usually through "good deeds" or observance of the law, are as filthy rags in God's eyes (Isaiah 64:6). Yet we may not come before Yahweh, God Almighty, in a state of spiritual nakedness or filthiness.

Christians believe that Yahweh Himself is the only One capable of clothing fallen humanity in the spotlessly white spiritual garment of His own righteousness, the only garment acceptable in His sight and one that He alone can provide. This is the righteousness of Jesus His Son, in which He will enfold every Christian believer as he or she comes into His holy presence.[14]

The Effects of the Fall

People all over the world and throughout history live in the dark shadow of the outcome of the fall. Roland Muller, in his book *Honor and Shame*,[15] describes three main negative effects of the fall upon man: guilt, shame, and fear. Although all three are present in all cultures, some people groups show tendencies to emphasize one over the others.

Much of the English-speaking world and parts of Europe are "guilt-based" cultures. People are held accountable to a standard of behavior developed by mutual agreement among their citizens and codified as civic law. Governments of guilt-based cultures recognize violations of the agreed-upon standard, determine guilt or innocence according to established procedures, and apply justice and mercy accordingly.

For instance, most Western civic law is taken from the religious doctrinal backgrounds of national "founding fathers." Many of the citizens of these democratic republics don't even realize (or prefer to ignore) the reality that Biblical Christianity formed the bedrock foundation of their law and government.

But Christianity is a *belief* system, not a prescribed form of government. Christianity brings about social change through the regeneration of individual hearts. Biblical Christians are given the grace and strength to govern themselves and thereby sustain a peaceful and just society. Laws in countries where Christians predominate are inspired by the guidance contained in the Holy

Bible, but are not synonymous with it. There are very few, if any, nations that call themselves "The Christian Republic of. . . ."

On the other hand, for Qur'anic Muslims, the very foundation for civil jurisprudence is the Noble Qur'an itself. National law is "shari'ah law." The Hadith and Sunnah of the Prophet are also used to develop rules and regulations. Government and Islam go hand-in-hand. A nation embracing Muslim law often labels itself "The Islamic Republic of. . . ."

The determination of guilt or innocence in nations with Biblical Christian roots is accomplished through an impartial and separate judicial court system. In Islamic republics, it is done through clerical edict supported by state power. This is a very, very big difference.

But guilt was not the only outcome of sin in the garden of Eden. When the first man and woman realized they had sinned, they immediately hid themselves (Genesis 3:8). They were ashamed. Predominantly shame-based cultures span an area from Morocco to Korea. The Noble Qur'an is full of references to shame.

In Islamic cultures, the primary focus of each individual is to avoid shame by whatever means possible. People use many techniques, including deceit, hypocrisy, pretentiousness, and rumor. The end justifies the means. One's reputation and standing in the community, personal honor, and family pride must not be compromised. Adherence to an internal moral standard or an external rule is far less important than presenting oneself in a good light to others. In the end, it's often a game of smoke and mirrors.

Muslim communities are strongly shame-based, and this has had devastating consequences for women. In Islamic belief and practice, tremendous pressure is applied to Muslim women, who are seen as the guardians of honor for their entire family and, consequently, the broader community.

Her sexuality is often the main focus of control:

What is honor? Abeer Allam, a young Egyptian journalist, remembered how it was explained by a high-school biology teacher as he sketched the female reproductive system and pointed out the entrance to the vagina.

"This is where the family honor lies!" the teacher declared, as Allam remembers it.

More than pride, more than honesty, more than anything a man might do, female chastity is seen in the Arab world as an indelible line, the boundary between respect and shame. An unchaste woman, it is sometimes said, is worse than a murderer, affecting not just one victim, but her family and her tribe.[16]

Muslim men spend a lot of energy tightly guarding and controlling women. Women are veiled, isolated, watched, chaperoned, and burdened with many other regulatory practices, some of which are ultimately dangerous to their health and safety. In short, a woman's freedom is severely curtailed, and ever her life may be taken, in the name of preserving a façade of "honor."

The third influence of sin was dread and fear of God. Before this, the man and woman "feared" God in the sense of having deep respect for Him. But after the fall their fear became bone-shaking terror. Fallen man cowered and hid from His presence. He still does.

Fear-based cultures are found mostly in Africa, Central and South America, and some islands in the Far East. These cultures are characterized by superstition, ritual, and spiritism. Fear-based people groups develop elaborate ceremonies and rites to protect themselves from unseen dangers, real or imagined. They employ taboos, amulets, charms, spells, and sacrifices to win favor from "good" forces and foil "bad" ones. People are in a constant power-struggle with darkness and the spirit world. These cultures are often technologically and socially primitive. Fear paralyzes their ability to grow and advance.

Islam also has characteristics of fear-based theology, especially in folk or popular Islam. Muslim women in many Eastern cultures today are deeply caught up in occult practices.[17] The promise of power is irresistible to those who are truly powerless in their own cultures. (The bibliography at the end of this book includes resources that discuss this topic in greater detail.)

THE BOTTOM LINE

Through strict adherence to the "guidance"[18] provided in shari'ah law and all its attendant rites, rituals, and obligations, modern Muslims are "saved" from being seduced by evil in this life and are promised many sensual rewards in the next life. "A life narrowed down"[19] is used as a description of the personal consequences of rejecting Allah's guidance in the Noble Qur'an.

But the truth is: the phrase is more strikingly applied primarily to women under Islam.

Two

Creation and the Fall in the Holy Bible

We have seen what the Noble Qur'an says about the creation of mankind. And we have noted that it differs from what the Holy Bible reveals. But what, actually, does the Bible teach about creation and the rebellion of Satan and humanity, and the result thereof for man and woman?

The Holy Bible is assembled more chronologically than the Noble Qur'an. The very first book of the Holy Bible describes the creation of man and woman in this way:

Genesis 1:26–28

> Then God said, "Let us make man in our image, after our likeness. And let them have dominion over the fish of the sea and over the birds of the heavens and over the livestock and over all the earth and over every creeping thing that creeps on the earth."
>
> So God created man in his own image,
> in the image of God he created him;
> male and female he created them.

And God blessed them. And God said to them, "Be fruitful and multiply and fill the earth and subdue it and have dominion over the fish of the sea and over the birds of the heavens and over every living thing that moves on the earth."

Genesis 2:7–25

Then the LORD God formed the man of dust from the ground and breathed into his nostrils the breath of life, and the man became a living creature. And the LORD God planted a garden in Eden, in the east, and there he put the man whom he had formed. And out of the ground the LORD God made to spring up every tree that is pleasant to the sight and good for food. The tree of life was in the midst of the garden, and the tree of the knowledge of good and evil.

A river flowed out of Eden to water the garden, and there it divided and became four rivers. The name of the first is the Pishon. It is the one that flowed around the whole land of Havilah, where there is gold. And the gold of that land is good; bdellium and onyx stone are there. The name of the second river is the Gihon. It is the one that flowed around the whole land of Cush. And the name of the third river is the Tigris, which flows east of Assyria. And the fourth river is the Euphrates.

The LORD God took the man and put him in the garden of Eden to work it and keep it. And the LORD God commanded the man, saying, "You may surely eat of every tree of the garden, but of the tree of the knowledge of good and evil you shall not eat, for in the day that you eat of it you shall surely die."

Then the LORD God said, "It is not good that the man should be alone; I will make him a helper fit for him." So out of the ground the LORD God formed every beast of the field and every bird of the heavens and brought them to the man to see what he would call them. And whatever the man called every living creature, that was its name. The man gave names to all livestock and to the birds of the heavens and to every beast of the field. But for Adam there was not found a helper fit for him. So the LORD God caused a deep sleep to fall upon the man, and while he slept took one of his ribs and closed up its place with flesh. And the rib that the LORD God had taken from the man he made into a woman and brought her to the man. Then the man said,

> "This at last is bone of my bones
>   and flesh of my flesh;
> she shall be called Woman,
>   because she was taken out of Man."

Therefore a man shall leave his father and his mother and hold fast to his wife, and they shall become one flesh. And the man and his wife were both naked and were not ashamed.

CREATION OCCURRED IN A DEFINED ORDER

Although the Biblical God, Yahweh, exists above and beyond time, He created all things within and over time. Everything was not created simultaneously. First, God created the earth, then the skies, then the seas. Next, by the power of His infinite word, He brought into being animal and plant life in all of its amazing variety and richness. He pronounced it all "good" and commanded all created living things to grow and reproduce after their own kind upon the face of the earth.

As the crown of creation, God made man. He did this in a way unlike any other creative act. Yahweh used unique words with unique intent.

"Let *us* make man in *our* image, after *our* likeness..." (Genesis 1:26).

Us... Our image... Our likeness.

Yahweh is magnificent and majestic—there is no being like Him in the entire universe (see Psalm 86:8; Isaiah 46:9). He is highly exalted, pure, and holy. He exists in "complex unity" (see Appendix) as an eternal, loving, relational God in three persons: the Father, the Son, and the Holy Spirit.

The three persons of the Triune God love one another intensely and eternally. They are in complete agreement with one another and are united in purpose. Each possesses all the attributes of divinity (see Appendix).

Scripture confirms that each of the persons of the triune God fulfills a specific role. There is no power struggle or conflict between them. The person of the Son, Jesus, performs His role of the redemption of mankind in submission to the Father. The person of the Holy Spirit calls and sanctifies believers in submission to the Son and the Father. This submission is not a mark of inferior status, but is a sign of singular focus and mutual devotion.

When the Holy Bible describes God as giving human beings His image and likeness, it is explaining that He is blessing them in an absolutely unique way. He is making them into relational beings like Himself. As such, they "both mirror and represent God."[1] Simply put, this means that every aspect of the humanity and personality of the first created man and woman bore the special imprint of God. Each was infused with equal measures of His image and likeness. Neither received more or less of His image than the other.

It is also important to understand what the image and likeness of God is *not* when applied to mankind. It is not divinity. It is not the fullness of His being. It is not omniscience, omnipotence, or omnipresence. Man is *not* God, nor will he ever be God, or even "a god." The Biblical Yahweh is the one and only true God. He always was, always is, and always will be. In fact, that is what the name "Yahweh" means: He who was, and is, and is to come.

BIBLICAL COMPLEMENTARIANISM

It was Yahweh's good pleasure to create man as both male and female. And in this Scripture is clear: God chose to create the male human being *first*. He created him directly from the raw ingredients of created earth—the dust of the ground. The woman, by contrast, was created *after* the man, *from* the man, and *for* the man.

The first woman was built from the rib of Adam and was truly bone of the man's bones and flesh of the man's flesh (see Genesis 2:23). God created her to be Adam's perfect teammate, helper, and companion. Both the man and the woman manifested the image and likeness of Yahweh *within and through their respective masculinity and femininity*.

The man was given the responsibility to lead the pair in the performance of their singular purpose: to exercise stewardship over the earth. The woman was created to give willing assistance to the man's loving leadership *following the relational pattern of the triune God Himself*. She is in submission to the man in the same way that the persons of the Godhead are in submission. Therefore, submission to the leadership of the man did not diminish the woman's "personhood" in any way. She was fully human, reflecting the image and likeness of Yahweh in her femaleness, wholeheartedly committed to the accomplishment of the God-given task set before them.

This Biblical view of godly gender relationships is called "complementarianism." Dr. John Piper, well-known Christian pastor and writer, describes it this way:

> Complementarity means that the music of our relationships should not be merely the sound of singing in unison. It should be the integrated sound of soprano and bass, alto and tenor. It means that the differences of male and female will be respected and affirmed and valued. It means that male and female will not try to duplicate each other, but will highlight in each other the unique qualities that make for mutual enrichment.[2]

This "mutual enrichment" is most efficiently accomplished by the differentiation of roles:

Now God wants to say something more about the relationship between man and woman. And what He wants to say is that when it comes to their differing responsibilities there is a "firstness" of responsibility that falls to the man. This is not an issue of superior value. That issue has been settled in Genesis 1:27. It's an issue of a sinless man, in childlike dependence on God, being given a special role or responsibility. God makes him lead the way into being to say something about his responsibility of leadership. . . .

The second observation to make is this: One of the responsibilities that came with being there first was the primary responsibility (not the only, but the primary responsibility) to receive and teach and be accountable for the moral pattern of life in the garden of Eden.[3]

THE "HEADSHIP" OF MAN

A table titled "Theological Foundations for Headship" on page 6 of the *Women's Study Bible*[4] describes the scriptural basis for the man's leadership. The information in this table is summarized below:

- The priority of Adam's creation. (Genesis 2:7)
- The use of the name "Adam" for the entire race. (Genesis 2:20)
- The investiture of Adam, with authority prior to Eve's creation. (Genesis 2:15)
- The assignment to the man of the responsibility for provision and protection. (Genesis 2:15–17)
- The responsibility of the man in naming the animals. (Genesis 2:20)
- The designation of the woman as the man's helper. (Genesis 2:18, 20)
- The naming of the woman by the man. (Genesis 2:23; 3:20)
- The recognition of the man as leader and spokesman. (Genesis 3:9, 11)

This view comes into direct conflict with contemporary secular feminist thought. The image of womanhood portrayed in popular culture is *not* an accurate representation of the Biblical view of Christian womanhood. *Biblical Christians reject radical and extreme views of secular feminism.*

In addition, there is a deep misconception throughout the Muslim world that all Western women are "Christian" women. It is inaccurate to equate the image of Western secular women presented in films and other mainstream media with the true behavior of women within contemporary and God-honoring Biblical Christianity. The images are as different as night and day!

God-fearing Christians know that it is not popular within secular liberal society these days to say that men were created to lead. It is not popular to say that women were created to help. It offends the individualistic, me-centered, "be-your-own-person" mentality to think that women should find satisfaction, purpose, or honor in a complementarian role.

It is not popular because we are all *fallen*.

THE FALL OF HUMANITY

Genesis 2:15–17

> The LORD God took the man and put him in the garden of Eden to work it and keep it. And the LORD God *commanded the man,* saying, "You may surely eat of every tree in the garden; but of the tree of the knowledge of good and evil you shall not eat, for in the day that you eat of it you shall surely die."

Genesis 3:1–7

> Now the serpent was more crafty than any other beast of the field that the LORD God had made.
> He said *to the woman,* "Did God actually say, 'You shall not eat of any tree in the garden'?" And the woman said

to the serpent, "We may eat of the fruit of the trees in the garden, but God said, 'You shall not eat of the fruit of the tree that is in the midst of the garden, *neither shall you touch it*, lest you die.' " But the serpent said to the woman, "You will not surely die. For God knows that when you eat of it your eyes will be opened, and you will *be like God*, knowing good and evil." So when the woman saw that the tree was *good for food, and that it was a delight to the eyes, and that the tree was to be desired to make one wise*, she took of its fruit and ate, and she also gave some to her husband *who was with her*, and he ate. Then the eyes of both were opened, and they knew that they were naked. And they sewed fig leaves together and made themselves loincloths.

Yahweh's command to not eat of the Tree of the Knowledge of Good and Evil occurs in the narrative *before* the creation of the woman. There is no scriptural evidence that Yahweh repeated His command to both of them at a later time. It is reasonable to conclude that the woman received information about the forbidden tree *only from the man*, not personally or directly from Yahweh.

It was the man's responsibility to lead the woman in obedience—not by force, but by teaching and example. This required the man to relate Yahweh's instruction clearly and accurately, demonstrate his adherence to it, and assist her in their mutual honoring of God's Word. If the man failed in any part of this task, the woman would be vulnerable. And if she became vulnerable, so would he.

And Satan knew this:

> Now Satan knows that this [pattern of moral leadership] is a beautiful arrangement. He knows that God's pattern of life is designed for man's good. But Satan hates God and he hates man. He is a liar and a killer from the beginning. And so what does he do? . . .
>
> Satan assaults God's pattern by attacking the woman instead of the man.[5]

The original interaction between mankind and animals must have been one of peaceful coexistence. The woman is not reported to have felt any apprehension, surprise, or dismay during her encounter with the serpent or the fact that they were having a conversation. Indeed, there is nothing in the description of the garden to imply anything other than total compatibility between the creatures of Yahweh's garden, including created man.

When Satan began talking to the woman, he first cast doubt upon the clearly revealed Word of God. He likes this tactic. It is very, very effective. He still uses it today.

Notice that in verse 3, when the woman recites Yahweh's command (which she did not actually hear), she adds the phrase "neither shall you touch it." This simple alteration turned the basic law given by God into something much more restrictive. Satan loves it when human beings do this today, too. It makes him bold. He knows it is just a short hop from "adding" to "contradicting."

First, Satan cunningly used partial truth to entice the woman to disobedience. Then he directly refuted God's statement about the consequences of man's disobedience with the assertion, "You will not surely die." He twisted the truth just enough to encourage the woman to consider the fruit and give full rein to her sense of taste and sight, which, in turn, incited desire in her heart and mind.

It was true that the fruit brought the knowledge of good and evil. It was true that this was certainly "like God." But Satan did not tell her the *whole* truth. He did not tell her that the fruit would not provide the ability to discern the difference between good and evil. Nor would it give them the spiritual strength to choose the good over the evil. *Simple knowledge of or about good and evil is totally insufficient to make one wise.*

DESIRE FOR WISDOM

True wisdom is the wisdom of God that gives us the ability to apply knowledge in a righteous way to glorify Him and further His purpose and kingdom. It is acquired over time through a close, loving relationship with Him. It is fed by the study of, meditation upon, and application of, the Word of God contained in the Holy Bible. Tidbits of information and chunks of mere facts may be grasped with relative swiftness, but there are no quick "downloads" of wisdom.

Yahweh desires that men and women enjoy the benefit of His holy wisdom (see Psalms 51:6; 111:10; Proverbs 1:2; 8:11; 9:10). Indeed, His Word instructs us to value wisdom (see Job 28:18) and *ask Him* for it (see James 1:5). But the first woman was persuaded that she should not wait upon Yahweh for it, rely on His provision of it, or depend on His perfect timing to grow in it. Instead she was led by Satan to believe that she should simply reach out and take it by her own strength and according to her own will. Satan's strategy was (and still is) to stir up discontent in human hearts and minds and to convince men and women to take by our own effort what we think is "good" in our flawed human judgment. We think we need not wait for Him to supply what is best for us. In essence, we rebel against His perfect provision.

REBELLION

God created the man and woman with the capacity for rebellion. Some call it "free will," others label it "choice." Satan turned this capacity for rebellion into *inclination toward* rebellion, knowing that the end result would be *bondage to* rebellion. The great reformer Martin Luther wrote an entire treatise based on this truth, aptly titled "The Bondage of the Will."

So the woman took the fruit into her own hands and tasted it. When she made that choice, *the man was with her.* Scripture does not record his participation in the discussion, his counsel to the woman (if any), his reaction or response to Satan. The facts are these: the woman tasted the fruit, presented it to him, and he ate.

The woman did not enter the fallen state before the man. The man did not observe for a while the effects of the fruit upon her and then elect to join her out of compassion or obligation. The tragic corruption in their natures occurred *after they both had eaten the fruit.* The mutual commission of the forbidden deed seals their fate. They were "one flesh"; they were in it together. The same consequences come to both of them at the same time from the same disobedient act.

Suddenly and frightfully, their eyes were opened to knowledge, but their true desire, wisdom, did not follow.

Mankind fell.

CONSEQUENCES OF THE FALL

Genesis 3:8–13

> And they heard the sound of the LORD God walking in the garden in the cool of the day, and the man and his wife hid themselves from the presence of the LORD God among the trees of the garden. But the LORD God called to the man and said to him, "Where are you?" And he said, "I heard the sound of you in the garden, and I was afraid because I was naked, and I hid myself." He said, "Who told you that you were naked? Have you eaten of the tree of which I commanded you not to eat?" The man said, "The woman whom you gave to be with me—she gave me fruit of the tree, and I ate." Then the LORD God said to the woman, "What is this that you have done?" The woman said, "The serpent deceived me, and I ate."

Yahweh's delight was to go to the garden to spend time in His creation with the man and the woman. The significance of this should not be overlooked. *The great God of the universe, Yahweh, delighted in human beings. He takes the initiative to seek out His own.* That evening He found two frightened rebels, recoiling from Him in dread and shame, hiding among the trees. What a foolish response—as if the God of the universe would not know where they were and what they had done! Instead of becoming wise, they had actually become quite silly.

God inquires, "Where are you?" Did He not know what had happened, what they had done, and how it occurred? Of course,

He did! But God was leading man into a precious thing: confession. The man gave Him an excuse instead.

The blame game—we have been playing it ever since. We cry that we are just "victims of circumstances!" We were misled; we didn't know; we were seduced! We attempt to fool others and ourselves into thinking that we can avoid culpability by "pointing the finger," shamelessly blaming our sins on someone else.

And that first "someone" was the woman.

Not only did the man single her out for the blame, but he tried to insinuate that the entire episode was *God's* fault by referring to her as "the woman *you* put here with me . . ."!

But she played the game too. She pointed to the serpent.

The serpent wasn't even given an opportunity to respond. Yahweh, knowing Satan's culpability and the serpent's role as a tool of Satan, pronounced judgment upon that creature immediately.

Genesis 3:14–15

> So the LORD God said to the serpent,
>
> "Because you have done this,
>   cursed are you above all livestock
>   and above all beasts of the field.
> on your belly you shall go,
>   and dust you shall eat
>   all the days of your life.
> I will put enmity between you and the woman,
>   and between your offspring and her offspring;
> he shall bruise your head,
>   and you shall bruise his heel."

JUDGMENT AND CURSE

Each judgment of Yahweh following the fall removed blessing from some aspect of creation, leading to an increased burden upon each creature and, consequently, upon the whole earth. Judgment upon the serpent is in the form of a curse, which takes something precious away from it. The serpent was literally "grounded." Today, it slithers about on the earth. Its original ability to walk upright, climb, or fly is gone. It eats dust. It is, to this day, a feared and reviled creature.

After Satan's deception, the gentle relationship that had existed between man and the creatures was undone. In its place is enmity and strife, including physical violence between men and beasts. The creatures of earth now fear, hunt, and harm one another.

(In Biblical Christianity, the symbolic nature of the enmity between the seed of woman and Satan is seen as a foreshadowing of redemption. The act of redemption accomplished by Jesus Christ, born of the virgin Mary, permanently destroyed Satan's power of bondage over believers. Satan may have bruised Christ's heel, but He has crushed Satan's head!)

Yahweh next turns His attention to the woman.

Genesis 3:16

To the woman he said,

> "I will surely multiply your pain in childbearing;
> in pain you shall bring forth children."

The original blessing of procreation, mandated *before* the fall of man, is now accompanied by sorrow. Yahweh graciously permitted the continuation of the human race, but withdrew the ease of childbirth. Consequently, women experience physical suffering during what is the most miraculous and joyful process known to man—the birth of a new human being.

Now we come to the punishment causing all of the difficulties between men and women. God withdrew the full blessing of perfect communion and compatibility between the sexes.

Genesis 3:16

> "Your desire shall be for your husband,
> and he shall rule over you."

Let's look back briefly before we look ahead. People are needy; God is not. Yahweh does not need man; He is wholly sufficient unto Himself. It was His good pleasure to create man for His own glory and delight. He provided for all human needs in the garden, including the opportunity to eat of the Tree of Life. This tree had not been forbidden to them and would have enabled them to live forever in delightful fellowship with Him.

Yahweh is glorified by the praise and worship of His people and their wholehearted devotion to Him in all things. The desire to love and delight in God alone (for only He is worthy of such love and delight!) is part of His own image and likeness. He is the Ultimate Delight, and choosing Him above all is the most exalted and perfect choice men and women can make. Living forever and ever in the personal presence of this amazing, wonderful, compassionate God *is meant to be man's highest purpose and greatest desire.*

Notice that God describes the corruption of the woman's desire in verse 17. It was, indeed, a great crime against Him that man pursued his desire for wisdom in an unrighteous and forbidden way, spurning God's provision. Divine justice demands that the consequences fit the crime. Therefore, God turned the woman over to her fallen and corrupt desire, a desire that is no longer directed toward Him, but toward her husband.

It is a description of misery, not a model for marriage. This is the way it's going to be in history where sin has the upper hand. But what is really being said here? What is the nature of this ruined relationship after sin?

The key comes from recognizing the connection between the last words of this verse (3:16b) and the last words of Genesis 4:7. Here God is warning Cain about his resentment and anger against Abel. God tells him that sin is about to get the upper hand in his life. Notice at the end of the verse 7: "Sin is crouching at the door; its desire is for you, but you must master it (literally: you shall rule over it)."

The parallel here between 3:16 and 4:7 is amazingly close. The words are virtually the same in Hebrew, but you can see this in the English as well. In 3:16 God says to the woman, "Your desire is for your husband, and he shall rule over you." In 4:7 God says to Cain, "Sin's desire is for you, and you shall [if you choose] rule over it."

Now the reason this is important to see is that it shows us more clearly what is meant by "desire." When 4:7 says that sin is crouching at the door of Cain's heart (like a lion, Genesis 49:9) and that its desire is for him, it means that sin wants to overpower him. It wants to defeat him and subdue him and make him the slave of sin.

Now when we go back to 3:16 we should probably see the same meaning in the sinful desire of woman. When it says, "Your desire shall be for your husband," it means that when sin has the upper hand in woman she will desire to overpower or subdue or exploit man. And when sin has the upper hand in man he will respond in like manner and with his strength subdue her, or rule over her.[6]

RULE VS. LEADERSHIP

Rule over something or someone is not necessarily the same thing as leadership, just as politicians are not the same as statesmen. Leadership is wise guidance that inspires others toward voluntary dedication to a mutually beneficial goal. Rule, on the other hand, can often deteriorate into independent and external control, sometimes motivated by greed or lust for power. Man's rule, now fallen and alienated from the sanctifying grace of God, is a heavy-handed corruption of the original blessing of godly leadership.

And it is as much of a burden for the man as it is for the woman!

When sin entered the world it ruined the harmony of marriage NOT because it brought headship and submission into existence, but because it twisted man's humble, loving headship into hostile domination in some men and lazy indifference in others. And it twisted woman's intelligent, willing submission into manipulative obsequiousness in some women and brazen insubordination in others. Sin didn't create headship and submission; it ruined them and distorted them and made them ugly and destructive.[7]

So what is really described in the curse of 3:16 is the ugly conflict between the male and female that has marked so much of human history. Maleness as God created it has been depraved and corrupted by sin. Femaleness as God created it has been depraved and corrupted by sin. The essence of sin is self-reliance and self-exaltation. First in rebellion against God, and then in exploitation of each other.[8]

Tragically, rather than being oriented toward God as in the beginning, the man and woman were both turned toward one another—not in complete harmony, but in opposition. Complete satisfaction, total compatibility, and perfect fulfillment within the original marriage covenant—designed and bestowed as a delightful blessing from the hand of God—was shattered.

Genesis 3:17–19

And to Adam he said,

> "Because you have listened to the voice of your wife
> > and have eaten of the tree of which I commanded you,
> 'You shall not eat of it,'
> cursed is the ground because of you;
> > in pain you shall eat of it all the days of your life;

> thorns and thistles it shall bring forth for you;
>> and you shall eat the plants of the field.
> By the sweat of your face
>> you shall eat bread,
> till you return to the ground,
>> for out of it you were taken;
> for you are dust,
>> and to dust you shall return."

The simple fact that the man listened to his wife was not the critical issue. The Holy Bible does not reject the idea of men heeding the advice of their wives. In fact, there are quite a few recorded instances in which wives have been commended for their sound and invaluable counsel to their husbands (see I Samuel 25; the book of Esther, Matthew 27:19).

But in the case of the fall, "the man was listening when he should have been leading."[9] What the woman thought, decided, and acted upon had been clearly contrary to what God had revealed to the man. As the moral leader of the team, he had the responsibility to reaffirm the original commandment God had delivered to him.

Now came another curse, and it was not on the man, but on the ground. (In fact, only the serpent and the ground were directly cursed. However, both curses certainly adversely affected both the man and the woman.)

The man retained stewardship of creation, but no longer will the task be the full blessing it was in the beginning. Like the childbearing of the woman, his personal labor and service is now scarred with pain and difficulty. He will know the anguish of unfruitful toil, wasted effort, and nature working against him. He will know continual hardship and frustration, thorns and thistles. The footnote on this passage in the *New International Version Study Bible* states, "Instead of submitting to human beings, it [the earth] would resist and eventually swallow them. . . ."[10]

BANISHMENT AND RESTORATION

Genesis 3:20–24

> The man called his wife's name Eve, because she was the mother of all living. And the LORD God made for Adam and for his wife garments of skins and clothed them.
>   Then the LORD God said, "Behold, the man has now become like one of us in knowing good and evil. Now, lest he reach out his hand and take also of the tree of life and eat, and live forever—" therefore the LORD God sent him out from the garden of Eden to work the ground from which he was taken. He drove out the man, and at the east side of the garden of Eden he placed the cherubim and a flaming sword that turned every way to guard the way to the tree of life.

Yahweh's withdrawal of the right to eat of the Tree of Life was a gracious act under these circumstances. He refused to allow man to live forever in this fallen state. He will not tolerate an eternity of fallen men fearing and fleeing His holy and delightful presence.

But there is good news! He promises that the Tree of Life will be present in the new heaven and earth of the future. He promises that its fruit will once again be offered to His beloved and redeemed people, who will be clothed in the apparel of righteousness *He* provides. According to the Holy Bible, the perfect garment of righteousness belongs to Jesus Christ, God's precious Son (see Romans 3:21–26 and Philippians 3:9). Jesus will graciously spread its folds over each and every believer appearing before the Father on the day of judgment.

He desires that His chosen people should glorify and enjoy Him forever—and all that He desires will most assuredly come to pass. Until then, mankind may not dwell in the same place with the blessed tree. Yahweh actively drove the man and woman out of the garden, and the tree was hidden from them by divinely-appointed angelic barriers. They fled to the dry and barren wilderness away from God's immanent presence, to make their own way in a violent and inhospitable creation. They had declared their independence; now they were on their own.

They could not go back. God had blocked the way. Only God could open it again. . . .

Three

Men and Women in the Noble Qur'an

*L*et's briefly review some history. Muhammad had a passing familiarity with both ancient Judaism and emerging Christianity. However, much of what he learned was incomplete, heretical, or just downright wrong.[1] To further complicate matters, the culture of the Arabian Peninsula was an amalgamation of Bedouin and pre-Islamic tradition, superstition, and paganism, much of which found its way into the Noble Qur'an and the Hadith (sayings of the Prophet).

The Noble Qur'an is primarily a prescriptive document. Most of it is written in the imperative. It is a litany of "do this, don't do that": injunctions, warnings, laws, and precepts covering all areas of social, religious, and political life. These are punctuated by repetitive mantras to Allah. It is particularly specific in the area of "domestic law" and in social conventions controlling interactions between men and women.

Table 1 presents examples of injunctions related to contractual marriage. Pay particular attention to the italicized portions because they reveal the underlying misogynist viewpoint of the Qur'anic text.

TABLE 1: MARRIAGE IN THE NOBLE QUR'AN

2:221	Do not marry *unbelieving women (idolators)*, until they believe: a slave woman who believes is better than an unbelieving woman, even though *she allure you*. Nor marry your girls to unbelievers until they believe:
2:222	They ask thee concerning women's courses. Say: they are *a hurt and a pollution*: so keep away from women in their courses, and do not approach them until they are clean. But when they have purified themselves, *ye may approach them in any manner, time, or place* ordained for you by God.
2:231	*When* ye divorce women, and they fulfill the term of their ('Iddat), either take them back on equitable terms or set them free on equitable terms; but do not take them back to injure them, to take undue advantage; if anyone does that, he wrongs his own soul.
2:236	There is *no blame on you if ye divorce women* before consummation or the fixation of their dower; but bestow on them (a suitable gift) . . .
2:241	For divorced women maintenance (should be provided) on a reasonable (scale). This is a duty of the righteous.
4:3	*Marry women of your choice, two, or three, or four*; but if ye fear that ye shall not be able to deal justly (with them) [orphans], then only one, *or (a captive)* that your right hands possess.
4:4	And give the women (on marriage) their dower as a free gift; but if they, of their own good pleasure, *remit any part of it to you, take it and enjoy it with right good cheer.*
4:19	O ye who believe! Ye are forbidden to inherit women against their will. Nor should ye treat them with harshness, that ye may take away part of the dower ye have given them,—*except* where they have been guilty of open lewdness; on the contrary live with them on a footing of kindness and equity, *if ye take a dislike to them* it may be that you dislike a thing, and God brings about through it a great deal of good.
4:20	But if ye decide to *take one wife in place of another*, even if ye had given the latter a whole treasure for dower, take not the least bit of it back: would ye take it by slander and a manifest wrong?
4:34	Men are the protectors and maintainers of women, because *God has given the one more (strength) than the other*, and because they support them from their means. Therefore the righteous women are devoutly *obedient*, and guard in (the husband's) absence what God would have them guard. As to those women on whose part ye fear disloyalty and ill-conduct, admonish them (first), (next), refuse to share their beds, (and last) *beat them* (lightly) . . .

4:128	If a wife fears cruelty or desertion on her husband's part, there is no blame on them if they arrange an amicable settlement between themselves; and such settlement is best; even though *men's souls are swayed by greed.*
4:129	Ye are *never able to be fair and just* as between women, even if it is your ardent desire . . .
24:32	Marry those among you who are single, or the *virtuous ones among your slaves,* male or female: . . .
33:50	O Prophet! We have made *lawful to thee* thy wives to whom thou has paid their dowers; and those whom thy right hand possesses out of the prisoners of war whom God has assigned to thee; and daughters of thy paternal uncles and aunts, and daughters of thy maternal uncles and aunts, who migrated (from Mecca) with thee; and *any believing woman who dedicates her soul to the Prophet* if the Prophet wishes to wed her;—*this only for thee [Muhammad], and not for the believers (at large);* we know what we have appointed for them as to their wives and the captives whom their right hands possess;—in order that there should be no difficulty for thee.
33:51	*Thou mayest defer (the turn of)* any of them [Muhammad's wives] that thou pleasest, and thou mayest *receive any thou pleasest:* and there is no blame on thee if thou invite one whose (turn) thou hadst set aside. This were nigher to the cooling of their eyes, the prevention of their grief, and their satisfaction—. . .
33:52	It is not lawful for thee (to marry more) women after this, nor to change them for (other) wives, even though their beauty attract thee, *except* any thy right hand should possess (as *handmaidens*) . . .
60:10	O ye who believe! When there come to you believing women refugees, examine (and test) them: God knows best as to their faith: if ye ascertain that they are believers, then send them not back to the unbelievers. They are not lawful (wives) for the Unbelievers, nor are the (Unbelievers) lawful (husbands) for them.
65:1	O Prophet! When ye do divorce women, *divorce them at their prescribed periods,* and count (accurately) their prescribed periods; and fear [Allah] your Lord: and turn them not out of their houses, nor shall they (themselves) leave, except in case they are guilty of some open lewdness, those are limits set by [Allah]. . . .
65:4	Such of your women as have passed the age of monthly courses, for them the prescribed period, if ye have any doubts, is *three months,* and for those who have no courses (it is the same): For those who carry (life within their wombs), their period is until they deliver their burdens . . .

> 65:6 Let the women live (in 'Iddat) in the same style as ye live, according to your means: annoy them not, so as to restrict them. And if they carry (life in their wombs), then spend (your substance) on them until they deliver their burden: and if they suckle your (offspring), *give them their recompense*: and take mutual counsel together, according to what is just and reasonable. And if ye find yourselves in difficulties, let another woman suckle (the child) on the (father's) behalf.

MARRIAGE AS A CONTRACT

In Islam, marriage is primarily a *legal contract.* A contract is a mutually beneficial financial and/or legal arrangement between two parties. A contract is written with the underlying presupposition that default by one party or the other is a distinct possibility. Stipulations are designed to mitigate the consequences of such default.

Contracts usually include severe penalties for noncompliance, often in the form of financial compensation. Provisions are made for extraordinary circumstances. All of this is tediously described using ubiquitous "legalese." The Noble Qur'an reads like a legal document when it addresses the institution of marriage and is full of descriptions of divorce procedures and laws.

The character of Islamic marriage is painted in both broad ideological strokes and in meticulous detail. There are injunctions against marriage with unbelievers, sexual intercourse during a woman's menstrual period, unwarranted confiscation of dower (the husband's gift to her upon marriage), inheriting "unwilling" women, and women engaging in prayer in an unwashed state after intercourse. Within Islam, sexual contact with a woman, particularly a menstruating woman, renders a man unclean.

Men are the sowers of the seeds of the next generation and masters of their "fields."[2] Sexual intercourse should occur at his demand and in the way and place he prefers. Although he is counseled to be "considerate" of her, a wife is considered disobedient if she does not make herself available to him at all times. In chapter 4 we will see how the hadith reaffirm this male right.

Muslim men are also in control of divorce and reconciliation.[3] Iddat is a prescribed waiting period following the decision to divorce. Although Muslim apologists explain it as a "cooling off" period in which the partners are urged to reconcile, its original intention was solely to determine if the woman was pregnant or not, so the man could be held financially responsible for any offspring he may have "left behind." It lasts for "three courses," or three menstrual periods. If the woman is pregnant and the divorce is nonetheless finalized, there are further instructions regarding her "reasonable maintenance" (alimony and child support) after the birth of the baby.[4] While this may seem charitable on the surface, one must wonder why a man would be having sexual relations with his wife, and then, shortly afterward, demand a divorce. This hardly seems righteous.

Refugee and slave women are considered "free game" when it comes to acquiring additional wives from conquered populations, as well as Muslim women who are left widowed by war.[5] Women are to be examined physically and psychologically for their suitability for marriage and are regarded as another coveted thing to be possessed in abundance.[6]

Dress is a big issue, and it is incumbent upon the woman to cover herself up "properly" in whatever circumstance she finds herself.[7] She is restricted regarding to whom she may show herself. If she violates these rules by revealing anything considered inappropriate, she may be numbered among the "showy or unchaste women,"[8] a designation which could result in punishment, and certainly, loss of honor.

These guidelines for maintaining the "purity and good form of domestic life" are a large part of the means by which a Muslim earns his right to paradise.[9]

Muhammad is a privileged character in Islam. Although the general Muslim male is limited to four wives, Muhammad was given special permission to marry as many as he liked.[10] This number varies according to source. It is certain he had at least nine wives at one time, and some scholars attribute thirteen or more "marriages" to him. Others describe some of his liaisons as concubines. What is certain is that he enjoyed the sexual favors of a greater number of women than was permitted to the ordinary Muslim man.

Muslim men must not have favorite wives and must treat all of their wives equally.[11] This is why Saudi princes have so many homes, private jets, luxury vehicles, etc. Each wife and her household must be provided with exactly the same goods and services as all the other wives in order to maintain complete equality among them. This is extended to include sexual relations (which, in Muhammad's case, had to be tracked according to a rotational schedule). If any wife is perceived to be receiving less that that of another in any of these parameters, charges of favoritism can be leveled against the husband.

However, it is clear that emotional favoritism cannot be so easily controlled. Muhammad himself was unable to eliminate or conceal his favoritism for 'Aisha from his own group of wives, as we will see in the next chapter. And he was the paragon of Muslim virtue.

DIFFERENCES BETWEEN THE NOBLE QUR'ANIC AND BIBLICAL CHRISTIAN VIEWS OF MARRIAGE

Contrast Islamic marriage with the Biblical marital relationship outlined in the last chapter. The differences are startling. Totally absent in Islam is the Biblical theme of two becoming one flesh. In its place are injunctions legitimizing certain forms of punishment for wives. A man may take action against her if he merely "fears" her disobedience. He may admonish her (in the same manner as children); he may withdraw sexual intimacy from her to underscore his displeasure. Ultimately (as a "last resort" say Islamic scholars), he may physically abuse her—an appalling outcome even when "softened" by Ali's parenthetical addition of the word "lightly."

So, what's the point? The reality is that a societal or religious view of marriage extends well beyond each husband and wife. The character of a marriage determines the character of an entire family. The character of a collective group of families determines the character of the culture. And the character of a culture becomes the character of a nation—rippling across the international stage.

For example, each of the nineteen young men who carried out the attack against the United States on September 11, 2001, grew up in strong Muslim families embracing the principles described above. They all studied the Noble Qur'an diligently and applied its injunctions with fatal results. The same can be said for those who carry out suicide bombings today and who commit other cowardly acts of terrorist violence. While the rest of the world tries to remain politically correct by downplaying or outright ignoring the link between Islam and terrorism, investigation after investigation clearly reveals that Islamic terrorists consider themselves first and foremost "devout Muslims." And the primary nursery for devotion to Islam resides in the marital relationship.

The way men and women treat one another in their marriages naturally spills over into all other gender relationships in a culture. The Noble Qur'an contains a number of injunctions which are expanded to address and control the behavior of all females within the Islamic community.

TABLE 2: WOMEN IN THE NOBLE QUR'AN

2:228	And women shall have rights similar to the rights against them, according to what is equitable; but *men have a degree (of advantage) over them*. And God is exalted in power, wise.
3:14	Fair in the eyes of men is the love of *things they covet; women and sons*; heaped-up hoards of gold and silver; horses branded (for blood and excellence); and (wealth of) cattle and well-tilled land. Such are the *possessions* of this world's life. . . .
4:15	If any of your women are guilty of lewdness, take the evidence of four (reliable) witnesses from amongst you against them; and if they testify, *confine them to houses until death do claim them*, or God ordain for them some (other) way.
4:43	O ye who believe! *Approach not prayers* with a mind befogged . . . or *if ye have been in contact with women*, and ye find no water, then take for yourselves clean sand or earth, and rub therewith your faces and hands. For God doth blot out sins and forgive again and again.

24:31	And say to the believing women that they should *lower their gaze* and guard their modesty; that they should *not display their beauty and ornaments* except what (must ordinarily) appear thereof; that they should *draw their veils over their bosoms* and not display their beauty except to their husbands, their fathers, their husband's fathers, their sons, their husbands' sons, their brothers or their brothers' sons, or their sisters' sons, or their women, or their slaves whom their right hands possess, or male servants free of physical needs, or small children who have no sense of the *shame of sex*; and that they should not strike their feet in order to draw attention to their hidden ornaments.
24:60	Such elderly women as are past the prospect of marriage,—there is no blame on them if they lay aside their (outer) garments, provided they *make not a wanton display of their beauty:* but it is best for them to be modest: . . .
33:33	And *stay quietly in your houses*, and make not a dazzling display, like that of the former Times of Ignorance; and establish Regular Prayer, and give Regular Charity; and obey God in his Apostle.
33:59	O Prophet! Tell thy wives and daughters, and the believing women, that they should *cast their outer garments over their persons* (when abroad): that is most convenient, that *they should be known (as such) and not molested.*

The rules for veiling, staying in the home as much as possible, and remaining "modest" are here extended to all Muslim women, for the expressed purpose of protecting them from the unrighteous attentions of men.[12] Within Islam, men are considered to have so little self-control and are so lacking in the ability to behave with honor toward women that women must wear additional, and often burdensome, garments just to feel safe among them. It cannot be argued that the women were being protected from non-Muslims since the most oppressive veiling today is most vigorously maintained in countries where non-Muslim presence is practically non-existent.

If a woman is found guilty of sexual misconduct—and notice that it is *only the woman* to be punished—she is to be physically confined for an indefinite period of time.[13] Four witnesses are required for guilt to be ascertained, but this is a practical impossibility. In actual practice, a woman can be condemned by accusation alone. This kind of separation and confinement is called "purdah," and in some situations a woman can be forbidden to leave a specific room for the rest of her life if the authorities sentence her to it, or if they merely refuse to formally acquit her. A woman may also be required to observe purdah for other reasons if her husband deems it necessary.

Complete and total veiling is considered an extension of purdah in some very conservative Islamic cultures, and in many rural areas, since it maintains her social isolation beyond the confines of her home. Such a woman may move through the culture, silent and essentially unseen, never spoken to or touched, for most of her adult life.

The man's "degree of advantage" over women is affirmed. Ali's commentary explains this as the difference in "economic position,"[14] but we can see it is much more than that. One must ask why it is that in a society that claims to give women unprecedented freedoms and opportunities, women so often find themselves in an inferior economic position? This does not seem to have been the case in *pre-Islamic* Arabia. Before Muhammad "became" a prophet, he was hired and supported by his first wife, Khadija—a woman who had attained a high level of financial self-sufficiency and security within Arabic culture before the advent of Islam.

Many of the hadith, the sayings and practices of Muhammad, further expand the Qur'anic injunctions related to women. They also give us historical detail regarding his interactions with his wives. Let's now take a glimpse of Muhammad's home life.

Four

Women in the Hadith

Most of the information regarding Muhammad's domestic life comes from the recollections of family and associates, collectively known as the Hadith. According to various sources of the Hadith, Muhammad had between nine and thirteen wives. In the following tables, the narrator of each episode is listed, along with the volume and section where the information can be verified.

These quotations are extensive and are taken directly from the following website (emphasis has been added): http://www.sacred-texts.com/isl/bukhari/index.htm.

TABLE 3: HADITH REGARDING MUHAMMAD'S WIVES

The wives of Allah's Apostle were in two groups. One group consisted of 'Aisha, Hafsa, Safiyya and Sauda; and the other group consisted of Um Salama and the other wives of Allah's Apostle. The Muslims knew that *Allah's Apostle loved 'Aisha*, so if any of them had a gift and wished to give to Allah's Apostle, he would delay it, till Allah's Apostle had come to 'Aisha's home and then he would send his gift to Allah's Apostle in her home. The group of Um Salama discussed the matter together and decided that Um Salama should request Allah's Apostle to tell the people to send their gifts to him in whatever wife's house he was. Um Salama told Allah's Apostle of what they had	Narrated 'Urwa from 'Aisha: 3:755

said, but he did not reply. Then they (those wives) asked Um
Salama about it. She said, "He did not say anything to me."
They asked her to talk to him again. She talked to him again
when she met him on her day, but he gave no reply. When
they asked her, she replied that he had given no reply. They
said to her, "Talk to him till he gives you a reply." When it was
her turn, she talked to him again. He then said to her, "Do
not hurt me regarding 'Aisha, as the Divine Inspirations do
not come to me on any of the beds except that of 'Aisha." On
that Um Salama said, "I repent to Allah for hurting you."
Then the group of Um Salama called Fatima, the daughter of
Allah's Apostle and sent her to Allah's Apostle to say to him,
"*Your wives request to treat them and the daughter of Abu Bakr on equal terms.*"
Then Fatima conveyed the message to him. The Prophet said,
"O my daughter! Don't you love whom I love?" She replied in
the affirmative and returned and told them of the situation.
They requested her to go to him again but she refused. They
then sent Zainab bint Jahsh who went to him and used harsh
words saying, "Your wives request you to treat them and the
daughter of Ibn Abu Quhafa on equal terms." On that she
raised her voice and abused 'Aisha to her face so much so that
Allah's Apostle looked at 'Aisha to see whether she would
retort. 'Aisha started replying to Zainab till she silenced her.
The Prophet then looked at 'Aisha and said, "She is really the
daughter of Abu Bakr."

. . . on the authority of his father that he had asked 'Aisha about the saying of Ibn 'Umar (i.e., he did not like to be a Muhrim [forbidden] while the smell of scent was still coming from his body). 'Aisha said, "I scented Allah's Apostle and *he went round (had sexual intercourse with) all his wives*, and in the morning he was Muhrim (after taking a bath)."	Narrated Muhammad bin Al-Muntathir: 1:270 Buk
The Prophet used to *visit all his wives in one night* and he had nine wives at that time.	Narrated Anas bin Malik: 1:282 Buk
Anas bin Malik said, "The Prophet used to *visit all his wives in a round, during the day and night* and they were eleven in number." I asked Anas, "Had the Prophet the strength for it?" Anas replied, "We used to say that the Prophet was given the strength of thirty (men)." And Sa'id said on the authority of Qatada that Anas had told him about nine wives only (not eleven).	Narrated Qatada: 1:268 Buk

Dihya came and said, "O Allah's Prophet! Give me a slave girl from the captives." The Prophet said, "Go and take any slave girl." He took Safiya bint Huyai. A man came to the Prophet and said, "O Allah's Apostle! You gave Safiya bint Huyai to Dihya and she is the chief mistress of the tribes of Quraiza and An-Nadir and she befits none but you." So the Prophet said, "Bring him along with her." So Dihya came with her and when the Prophet saw her, he said to Dihya, "Take any slave girl other than her from the captives." Anas added: The Prophet then *manumitted her and married her.* I asked the Prophet, "Please ask Allah's forgiveness for me. The Prophet did not go to his wives because of the secret which Hafsa had disclosed to 'Aisha, and he said that he would not go to his wives for one month as he was angry with them when Allah admonished him (for his oath that he would not approach Maria). When twenty-nine days had passed, the *Prophet went to 'Aisha first of all.* She said to him, "You took an oath that you would not come to us for one month, and today only twenty-nine days have passed, as I have been counting them day by day." The Prophet said, 'The month is also of twenty-nine days." That month consisted of twenty-nine days.

Narrated 'Abdul 'Aziz: 1:367

By Allah, never is there a charming woman loved by her husband who has other wives, but *the women would forge false news about her.*
By Allah I never thought that Allah would reveal Divine Inspiration in my case, as I considered myself too inferior to be talked of in the Holy Qur'an. I had hoped that Allah's Apostle might have a dream in which Allah would prove my innocence. By Allah, Allah's Apostle had not got up and nobody had left the house before the Divine Inspiration came to Allah's Apostle. So, there overtook him the same state which used to overtake him, (when he used to have, on being inspired divinely). He was sweating so much so that the drops of the sweat were dropping like pearls though it was a (cold) wintry day. When that state of Allah's Apostle was over, he was smiling and the first word he said, " 'Aisha! Thank Allah, for Allah has declared your innocence." My mother told me to go to Allah's Apostle. I replied, "By Allah I will not go to him and will not thank but Allah." So Allah revealed: "Verily! They who spread the slander are a gang among you . . ." (24.11).

Narrated 'Aisha: 3:829

'Aisha further added "*Zainab was competing with me* (in her beauty and the Prophet's love), yet Allah protected her (from being malicious), for she had piety."

Narrated 'Aisha: 3:859

Women in the Hadith

Muhammad's household was characterized by the following:

- Rotation of Muhammad's sexual attentions according to a set schedule, which he could alter according to his personal desires.
- Veiling of Muhammad's wives to avoid recognition and interaction with men—which eventually was extended to all Muslim women in order to prevent their molestation by Muslim men (see Sura 33:59).
- Interaction with wives during their "unclean" period, which was not permitted to other "ordinary" believers.
- First choice in the selection of slave girls for additional marriages or to serve as concubines.
- Slander, jealousy, and competition among his wives (giving occasion for special revelation from Allah).
- Distinct favoritism shown toward specific wives, fueling jealousy and anxiety among them.

HADITH APPLICABLE TO ALL MUSLIM WOMEN

Muhammad made additional general statements regarding all women, which continue to be used to justify legal and social restrictions on female behavior and freedom. These hadith were accessed at the MSA-USC Hadith Database website located at http://www.usc.edu/dept/MSA/reference/searthhadith.html.

TABLE 4: HADITH REGARDING WOMEN UNDER ISLAM

Abu Huraira (Allah be pleased with him) reported: "Woman has been created from a rib and will in no way be straightened for you; so if you wish to benefit by her, benefit by her while *crookedness remains in her*. And if you attempt to straighten her, you will break her, and breaking her is divorcing her."	Sahih Muslim, 8:3467. See also Sahih Muslim 8:3466, 3468 and Sahih Bukhari vol. 7, book 62, no. 113.

Allah's Apostle said, "Treat women nicely, for a women is created from a rib, and the most curved portion of the rib is its upper portion, so, if you should try to straighten it, it will break, but if you leave it as it is, *it will remain crooked*. So treat women nicely."	Sahih Bukhari, vol. 4, book 55, no. 548. Narrated Abu Huraira.
Abu Huraira (Allah be pleased with him) reported Allah's Messenger (may peace be upon him) as having said: "A woman without a husband (or divorced or a widow) must not be married until she is consulted, and a virgin must not be married until her permission is sought." They asked the Prophet of Allah (may peace be upon him): "*How her (virgin's) consent can be solicited?*" He (the Holy Prophet) said: "*That she keeps silence.*"	Sahih Muslim, book 8, no. 3303.
That he had heard Hudhaifa saying, "Once I was sitting with 'Umar and he said, 'Who amongst you remembers the statement of Allah's Apostle about the afflictions?' I said, 'I know it as the Prophet had said it.' 'Umar said, 'No doubt you are bold.' I said, 'The *afflictions caused for a man by his wife*, money, children and neighbor are expiated by his prayers, fasting, charity and by enjoining (what is good) and forbidding (what is evil).' "	Sahih Bukhari, vol 1, book 10, no. 503. Narrated Shaqiq.
The Prophet said, "Isn't the witness of a woman equal half of that of a man?" The women said, "Yes." He said, "This is because of *the deficiency of the woman's mind.*"	Sahih Bukhari, vol. 3, book 48, no. 826. Narrated Abu Sai'id Al-Khudri.
The Prophet said, "I looked at Paradise and found poor people forming the majority of its inhabitants; and *I looked at Hell and saw that the majority of its inhabitants were women.*"	Sahih Bukhari, vol. 4, book 54, no. 464. Narrated 'Imran bin Husain.
The Prophet said: "I was shown the Hell-fire and that the majority of its dwellers were women who were ungrateful." It was asked, "Do they disbelieve in Allah?" (or are they ungrateful to Allah?) He replied, "*They are ungrateful to their husbands* and are ungrateful for the favors and the good (charitable deeds) done to them. If you have always been good	Sahih Bukhari, vol. 1, book 2, no. 28. Narrated Ibn 'Abbas: Hadith.

Women in the Hadith

(benevolent) to one of them and then she sees something in you (not of her liking), she will say, 'I have never received any good from you.' "

It is narrated on the authority of 'Abdullah b. 'Umar that the Messenger of Allah observed: "O womenfolk, you should give charity and ask much forgiveness for I saw you in bulk amongst the dwellers of Hell." A wise lady among them said: "Why is it, Messenger of Allah, that our folk is in bulk in Hell?" Upon this the Holy Prophet observed: "You curse too much and are ungrateful to your spouses. I have seen none *lacking in common sense and failing in religion* but (at the same time) robbing the wisdom of the wise, besides you." Upon this the woman remarked: "What is wrong with our common sense and with religion?" He (the Holy Prophet) observed: "Your lack of common sense (can be well judged from the fact) that the evidence of two women is equal to one man, that is proof of the lack of commonsense, and you spend some nights (and days) in which you do not offer prayer and in the month of Ramadan (during the days) you do not observe fast, that is a failing in religion."	Sahih Muslim, book 1, no. 142.
Once Allah's Apostle went out to the Musalla (to offer the prayer) o 'Id-al-Adha or Al-Fitr prayer. Then he passed by the women and said, "O women! Give alms, as I have seen that the majority of the dwellers of Hell-fire were you (women)." They asked, "Why is it so, O Allah's Apostle?" He replied, "You *curse frequently* and are ungrateful to your husbands. I have not seen anyone more *deficient in intelligence and religion* than you. A cautious sensible man could be led astray by some of you." The women asked, "O Allah's Apostle! What is deficient in our intelligence and religion?" He said, "Is not the evidence of two women equal to the witness of one man?" They replied in the affirmative. He said, "This is the deficiency in her intelligence. Isn't it	Sahih Bukhari, vol. 1, book 6, 301. Narrated Abu Said Al-Khudri.

true that a woman can neither pray nor fast during her menses?" The women replied in the affirmative. He said, "This is the deficiency in her religion."

The Prophet said, "Isn't the witness of a woman equal to half of that of a man?" The women said, "Yes." He said, "This is because of the deficiency of a woman's mind."	Sahih Bukhari, vol. 3, book 48, no. 826. Narrated Abu Said Al-Khudri.
The Prophet said, "Isn't it true that a woman does not pray and does not fast on menstruating? And that is the defect (a loss) in her religion."	Sahih Bukhari, vol. 3, book 31, no. 172. Narrated Abu Said.
Some women requested the Prophet to fix a day for them as the men were taking all his time. On that he promised them one day for religious lessons and commandments. Once during such a lesson the Prophet said, "A woman whose three children die will be shielded by them from the Hell-fire." On that a woman asked, "If only two die?" He replied, "Even two (will shield her from the Hell-fire)."	Sahih Bukhari, vol. 1, book 3, no. 101. Narrated Abu Said Al-Khudri: Hadith.
Whenever Allah's Apostle completed the prayer with Taslim, the women used to get up immediately and Allah's Apostle would remain at his place for some time before getting up. (The sub-narrator (Az-Zuhri) said, "We think, and Allah knows better, that he did so, so that the women might leave before men could get in touch with them)."	Sahih Bukhari, vol. 1, book 12, no. 829. Narrated Um Salama.
Had Allah's Apostle known what the women were doing, he would have forbidden them from going to the mosque as the women of Bani Israel had been forbidden.	Sahih Bukhari, vol. 1, book 12, no. 828. Narrated 'Aisha.
The Prophet said, "A woman should not travel for more than three days except with a Dhi-Mahram (i.e., a male with whom she cannot marry at all, e.g., her brother, father, grandfather, etc.) or her own husband."	Sahih Bukhari, vol. 2, book 20, no. 192. Narrated Ibn 'Umar.
Prophet (p.b.u.h) said, "It is not permissible for a woman who believes in Allah and the Last Day to travel for one day and night except with a Mahram."	Sahih Bukhari, vol. 2, book 20, no. 194. Narrated Abu Huraira.

The Prophet said, "A woman should not travel except with a Dhu-Mahram (her husband or a man with whom that woman cannot marry at all according to the Islamic Jurisprudence), and no man may visit her except in the presence of a Dhu-Mahram."	Sahih Bukhari, vol. 3, book 29, no. 85. Narrated Ibn 'Abbas.
That he heard the Prophet saying, "It is not permissible for a man to be alone with a woman, and no lady should travel except with a Mahram (i.e., her husband or a person whom she cannot marry in any case for ever; e.g., her father, brother, etc.)."	Sahih Bukhari, vol. 4, book 52, no. 250. Narrated Ibn Abbas.
Regarding the explanation of the following verse:—"If a wife fears Cruelty or desertion on her husband's part." (4.128) A man may dislike his wife and intend to divorce her, so she says to him, "I give up my rights, so do not divorce me."	Sahih Bukhari, vol. 3, book 43, no. 630. Narrated 'Aisha.
That he had asked 'Aisha about the meaning of the Statement of Allah: "If you fear that you shall not Be able to deal justly with the orphan girls, then marry (other) women of your choice, two or three or four." (4.3) She said, "O my nephew! This is about the orphan girl who lives with her guardian and shares his property. Her wealth and beauty may tempt him to marry her without giving her an adequate Mahr (bridal money) which might have been given by another suitor." So, such guardians were forbidden to marry such orphan girls unless they treated them justly and gave them the most suitable Mahr; otherwise they were ordered to marry any other woman. (4.127)	Sahih Bukhari, vol. 3, book 44, no. 674. Narrated 'Urwa bin Az-Zubair.
Allah's Apostle said, "He who has a slave-girl and educates and treats her nicely and then manumits and marries her, will get a double reward."	Sahih Bukhari, vol. 3, book 46, no. 720. Narrated Abu Musa.
The wife of Rifa'a Al-Qurazi came to the Prophet and said, "I was Rifa'a's wife, but he divorced me and it was a final irrevocable divorce. Then I married Abdur-Rahman bin Az-Zubair but he is impotent." The Prophet asked her "Do you want to remarry Rifa'a?	Sahih Bukhari, vol. 3, book 48, no. 807. Narrated 'Aisha.

You cannot unless you had a complete sexual relation with your present husband."	
That 'Aisha the wife of the Prophet told her uncle that once, while the Prophet was in her house, she heard a man asking Hafsa's permission to enter her house. 'Aisha said, "I said, 'O Allah's Apostle! I think the man is Hafsa's foster uncle.'" 'Aisha added, "O Allah's Apostle! There is a man asking the permission to enter your house." Allah's Apostle replied, "I think the man is Hafsa's foster uncle." 'Aisha said, "If so-and-so were living (i.e., her foster uncle) would he be allowed to visit me?" Allah's Apostle said, "Yes, he would, as the foster relations are treated like blood relations (in marital affairs)."	Sahih Bukhari, vol. 3, book 48, no. 814. Narrated Amra bint 'Abdur-Rahman.
The following verse: If a woman fears cruelty or desertion on her husband's part (i.e., the husband notices something unpleasant about his wife, such as old age or the like, and wants to divorce her, but she asks him to keep her and provide for her as he wishes). (4.128) "There is no blame on them if they reconcile on such a basis."	Sahih Bukhari, vol. 3, book 49, no. 859. Narrated 'Aisha.
I heard the Prophet saying, "Evil omen is in three things: The horse, the woman and the house."	Sahih Bukhari, vol. 4, book 52, no. 110 (also 111). Narrated 'Abdullah bin 'Umar.
Allah's Apostle said, "If a husband calls his wife to his bed (i.e., to have sexual relation) and she refuses and causes him to sleep in anger, the angels will curse her till morning."	Sahih Bukhari, vol. 4, book 54, no. 460. Narrated Abu Huraira.
Allah's Apostle said, "The first batch (of people) who will enter Paradise will be (glittering) like a full moon; and those who will enter next will be (glittering) like the brightest star. Their hearts will be as if the heart of a single man, for they will have no enmity amongst themselves, and everyone of them shall have two wives, each of whom will be so beautiful, pure and transparent that the marrow of the bones of their legs will be seen through the flesh. They will be glorifying Allah	Sahih Bukhari, vol. 4, book 54, no. 469. Narrated Abu Huraira.

in the morning and evening, and will never fall ill, and they will neither blow their noses, nor spit. Their utensils will be of gold and silver, and their combs will be of gold, and the fuel used in their centers will be the aloes-wood, and their sweat will smell like musk."

The Prophet said, "If anyone of you, on having sexual relation with his wife, says: 'O Allah! Protect me from Satan, and prevent Satan from approaching the offspring you are going to give me,' and if it happens that the lady conceives a child, Satan will neither harm it nor be given power over it."	Sahih Bukhari, vol. 4, book 54, no. 503. Narrated Ibn 'Abbas.

These hadith are self-explanatory, but to summarize:

- Women are "crooked"; they are beyond being "straightened" and for that reason must be treated condescendingly. This belief contrasts starkly to the Biblical mutual regard men and women ought to have for one another as co-heirs of the kingdom of God.
- Slave and captive women may be used for sexual release, i.e., raped. If a Muslim male decides to marry one, he gets a double reward from Allah.
- Women are an "affliction" and "evil omens," only endured and overcome by the ritualistic duties of Islam.
- Women's minds are "deficient," and they lack common sense.
- Women are by nature crude and ungrateful.
- Women are unable to practice all of the rites of Islam at the prescribed times due to their menses. They are required to "make up" the missed prayer and fasting at other times. Due to her other extensive responsibilities in the home, this becomes a practical impossibility, thereby causing defectiveness in her religion and righteousness.
- If a woman bears at least two children she can avoid conscription to hell—regardless of anything else about her character or submissiveness to Allah.

- Women may be verbally admonished and physically struck by men.
- Women are the ones primarily responsible for preventing interaction with men at the mosque by avoiding eye contact and physical proximity. This is why they are often required to pray in a separate part of the mosque.
- Women must always be accompanied in public by a male chaperone, whose qualifications are clearly defined. In some strongly Islamic nations, this law goes so far as to demand that grandmothers must be accompanied by their young grandsons (even if they are infants) in order to fulfill these requirements.
- Women may be divorced if their husbands dislike them for "something unpleasant," although she can appeal to him to keep her and offer to relinquish her property (dowry) to him to win his favor. Essentially, this amounts to bribing him so that she can avoid the dishonor she would incur if the man continues with the divorce.
- A man must atone for sexual contact with his wife during Ramadan, an act that renders him "unclean."
- Women are cursed until they submit to sexual intercourse with their husbands.
- Muslim men will each have at least two wives in Islamic Paradise (although some Islamic teaching states that seventy or more women await each man in the hereafter). These beings are translucent and ethereal, without any "unappealing" human habits or behaviors.
- An Islamic woman's reward (if any) in the hereafter is not specified.

Note that, originally, foster children were regarded as equal in familial standing to blood relatives, thereby making sexual relationships between family members and foster children incestuous and against the law. However, when Muhammad himself desired the wife of his foster son—who was legally, according to this definition, his daughter-in-law and off-limits to him, he conveniently received a revelation from Allah that abrogated this law in his case. This revelation was used to pressure Muhammad's foster son to divorce his wife and give her to Muhammad as a gift, which he accepted readily.

So, these statutes make us ask: In what way is Islam sexually egalitarian? These hadith provide the bedrock for many of the contemporary laws toward woman in all nations calling themselves "Islamic republics" around the world. Women are clearly not accorded the same human rights and freedoms applied to men. If they were, there would be no need for the myriad of news articles, human rights watch alerts, magazine feature stories, books, and other publications that draw attention to this blatant inequality.

Five

Men and Women in Biblical Christianity

*W*hy do men and women in cultures that have been influenced by Biblical teachings relate to each other in drastically different ways from men and women in Islamic cultures? We will examine, in this chapter and the next, the basic reasons.

Jesus lived his entire earthly life in the Middle East, and early Christianity developed in an Eastern cultural setting. As the good news about his death and resurrection was proclaimed throughout the region, it captured the hearts and minds of individuals from all walks of life and from all cultures, races, and ethnicities.

As Christianity spread north and west, its Eastern roots gave nourishment to Western flowers. But the blossoms can never be severed from their life-giving roots or they will surely die. Christianity in the West is the product of the confluence of Eastern and Western thought. It is a hybrid of the best of both worlds.

Western nations are not theocratic kingdoms. Although the United States is founded upon the principles of Biblical Christianity that were brought here by its early settlers and the founding fathers of its government, today's Western secular cultures (including those of Europe and North and South America) are not a product of one philosophy or religion, but of many. Citizens of most Western nations come from many backgrounds, cultures, ethnicities, and religions. A "typical" American's ancestry may be traced to many areas of the world.

What brings them all together, particularly in the United States, is an *idea*—the idea that people are free to think, feel, act, and worship according to their own consciences. Many freedoms contribute to this end: freedom of speech, freedom of assembly, freedom of religion. People exchange ideas in an atmosphere of mutual respect, and consensus is achieved through honest debate and free elections. These freedoms are balanced by the responsibility that each person has to control oneself and behave in a manner that will not infringe upon the rights and freedoms of others or threaten the safety and peace of the community.

This means that people in these cultures are free to pursue their own agendas within broadly defined limits. Sometimes a culture swings to one extreme or another. These days, it appears to those outside the culture that marriage doesn't seem to be taken seriously anymore. But, in fact, it is taken very seriously by those within the circle of true Biblical faith. Even though people are legally permitted by civil law in both Western secular and Eastern Muslim cultures to marry and divorce many, many times, Biblical Christians teach that this is not the ideal that God established.

MARRIAGE AS A COVENANT

In Biblical Christianity, marriage is a *covenant*. A covenant is a life-long commitment, based upon mutual affection, trust, and devotion. Those who enter a true covenant are bound together legally, emotionally, and spiritually. They want the best for one another and they desire to please one another. A covenant implies total commitment of heart, soul, mind, and spirit.

Covenants are God's idea. God Himself entered into covenants with men: Adam, Noah, Abraham, Isaac, Jacob, and Moses. These covenants were never taken lightly. Yahweh is a jealous God (see

Exodus 20:5; 34:14; Deuteronomy 4:24; 5:9; 6:15; Joshua 24:19). He will not share the heart of a person He has chosen with any other "god." His covenant with His chosen people is absolutely exclusive.

Exclusivity is also inherent in the Christian marriage covenant. *One* man shall leave his father and mother and cleave to his *one* wife. Henceforth, *two become one*. There is no room for another here, nor is there provision for separation. A man should not share his heart with any other woman, nor should a woman share her heart with any other man. Human beings, created in the image and likeness of God, are not animals. They were not created to consort with multiple partners.

The Old Testament of the Holy Bible describes the struggle between fallen men and women. Not all of this information is pleasant to read. To understand its purpose, one must know how to interpret Scripture properly.

The Holy Bible presents information in a variety of ways. Some is prescriptive, some is descriptive; some is historical, some is prophetic. Some passages give us examples for us to emulate, other passages describe situations we should avoid. It takes study and discernment to apply each passage appropriately. The main thing to be careful of is getting the two types of material mixed up: taking passages meant to be warnings and using them as examples for imitation!

Table 5 lists passages that describe the *positive* characteristics of a covenant of marriage among the early Hebrews. These are examples for emulation.

TABLE 5: MARRIAGE IN THE OLD TESTAMENT

Reference	Content	Characteristic
Genesis 24:67	Then Isaac brought her into the tent of Sarah his mother and took Rebekah, and she became his wife, and he loved her....	Loving

Reference	Content	Characteristic
Exodus 20:17	You shall not covet your neighbor's house; you shall not covet your neighbor's wife, or his male servant, or his female servant, or his ox, or his donkey, or anything that is your neighbor's.	Protective
Deuteronomy 17:17	And he shall not acquire many wives for himself, lest his heart turn away, nor shall he acquire for himself excessive silver and gold.	Exclusive
Deuteronomy 24:5	When a man is newly married, he shall not go out with the army or be liable for any other public duty. He shall be free at home one year to be happy with his wife whom he has taken.	Husband attentive to wife
1 Samuel 1:8	And Elkanah, her husband, said to her, "Hannah, why do you weep? And why do you not eat? And why is your heart sad? Am I not more to you than ten sons?"	Devoted to one another
Proverbs 5:18	Let your fountain be blessed, and rejoice in the wife of your youth.	Joyful
Proverbs 18:22	He who finds a wife finds a good thing and obtains favor from the LORD.	Good
Proverbs 19:14	House and wealth are inherited from fathers, but a prudent wife is from the LORD.	Provided by God
Song of Songs 7:10	I am my beloved's, and his desire is for me.	Sexually desired
Isaiah 54:5	For your Maker is your husband, the LORD of hosts is his name; the Holy One of Israel is your Redeemer, the God of the whole earth he is called.	Yahweh as husband of His people
Jeremiah 31:32	Not like the covenant that I made with their fathers on the day when I took them by the hand to bring them out of the land of Egypt, my covenant that they broke, though I was their husband, declares the LORD.	Yahweh as husband of His people

Reference	Content	Characteristic
Hosea 2:16	"And in that day," declares the LORD, "you will call me 'My Husband,' and no longer will you call me 'My Baal.'"	Yahweh as husband of His people
Malachi 2:15	So guard yourselves in your spirit, and let none of you be faithless to the wife of your youth.	Faithfulness

In table 5, Deuteronomy 17:17 may be of particular interest to Muslim readers. It alludes to the practice of polygamy in ancient times. While it is true that many of the Old Testament patriarchs had multiple wives, the New Testament teaches Biblical Christians that this was not Yahweh's perfect pattern as established at creation. Therefore, believers in Christ adhere to "one man, one woman" marriages.

GOD AS A HUSBAND

Repeated three times in the passages of table 5 is *Yahweh's description of Himself as the husband of His people*. He is our example of the perfect spouse. He is kind, forgiving, gentle, just, firm, and reliable. In the verse from the book of Hosea, He draws sharp contrast between a "Baal (master)" and a "husband." To "husband" someone is an ongoing act of love, not a perpetual demonstration of mastery.

This is analogous to the difference between leadership and rule. Baal ruled over idolaters, who created bizarre rituals and restrictive behaviors to demonstrate their devotion to him. He was a false god. Yahweh, by contrast, leads and guides His followers. He "husbands" them as the True God. Yahweh is teaching corrupt man something very important about leadership in these passages. Fallen man is inclined to wield his "rule" over women like a heavy club. Yahweh is teaching by example that a husband should trade the club for a caress. He is teaching men and women how to respond to one another in gentleness and humility, according to His original design.

The description of a wife who is flourishing under this kind of husband leadership is given in Proverbs 31:10–31:

An excellent wife who can find?
    She is far more precious than jewels.
The heart of her husband trusts in her,
    and he will have no lack of gain.
She does him good, and not harm,
    all the days of her life.
She seeks wool and flax,
    and works with willing hands.
She is like the ships of the merchant;
    she brings her food from afar.
She rises while it is yet night
    and provides food for her household
    and portions for her maidens.
She considers a field and buys it;
    with the fruit of her hands she plants a vineyard.
She dresses herself with strength
    and makes her arms strong.
She perceives that her merchandise is profitable.
    Her lamp does not go out at night.
She puts her hands to the distaff,
    and her hands hold the spindle.
She opens her hand to the poor
    and reaches out her hands to the needy.
She is not afraid of snow for her household,
    for all her household are clothed in scarlet.
She makes bed coverings for herself;
    her clothing is fine linen and purple.
Her husband is known in the gates
    when he sits among the elders of the land.
She makes linen garments and sells them;
    she delivers sashes to the merchant.
Strength and dignity are her clothing,
    and she laughs at the time to come.
She opens her mouth with wisdom,
    and the teaching of kindness is on her tongue.
She looks well to the ways of her household

> and does not eat the bread of idleness.
> Her children rise up and call her blessed;
> her husband also, and he praises her:
> "Many women have done excellently,
> but you surpass them all."
> Charm is deceitful, and beauty is vain,
> but a woman who fears the Lord is to be
> praised.
> Give her the fruit of her hands,
> and let her works praise her in the gates.

The excellent wife of a godly husband has the following characteristics: personal worth, trustworthiness, benevolence toward others, industriousness, dependability, business sense, intelligence, strength, compassion, generosity, confidence, dignity, hopefulness, diligence, blessedness, nobility, and praiseworthiness. Her entire family is graced by her character and fortitude. This is cause for great celebration and thanksgiving!

Yahweh did not finish His teaching with the Old Testament. Biblical Christians have an even more astonishing model. Yahweh *came to us* and demonstrated His truth to us in person, through His Son Jesus' compassionate ministry on earth.

JESUS AND WOMEN

The New Testament chronicles many of the interactions Jesus had with women during his earthly life.

TABLE 6: JESUS AND WOMEN IN THE GOSPELS

Reference	Content	Quality
Matthew 5:27, 31–32	You have heard that it was said, "You shall not commit adultery." But I say to you that everyone who looks at a woman with lustful intent has	Women respected, sanctity of marriage upheld

Reference	Content	Quality
	already committed adultery with her in his heart. . . . It was also said, "Whoever divorces his wife, let him give her a certificate of divorce." But I say to you that everyone who divorces his wife, except on the ground of sexual immorality, makes her commit adultery. And whoever marries a divorced woman commits adultery.	
Matthew 9:22	Jesus turned, and seeing her he said, "Take heart, daughter; your faith has made you well." And instantly the woman was made well.	Recognized women as God's daughters
Matthew 15:28	Then Jesus answered her, "O woman, great is your faith! Be it done for you as you desire." And her daughter was healed instantly.	Commended women for faith
Matthew 26:10	But Jesus, aware of this, said to them, "Why do you trouble the woman? For she has done a beautiful thing to me."	Defended and affirmed women
Matthew 27:55	There were also many women there, looking on from a distance, who had followed Jesus from Galilee, ministering to him.	Accepted women's ministry to him
Mark 7:26	Now the woman was a Gentile, a Syrophoenician by birth. And she begged him [Jesus] to drive the demon out of her daughter.	Welcomed women from foreign backgrounds
Luke 2:51	And he went down with them [his earthly parents, Joseph and Mary] and came to Nazareth and was submissive to them.	Honored his human mother
Luke 7:37–38	And behold, a woman of the city, who was a sinner, when she learned that he [Jesus] was reclining at table in the Pharisee's house, brought an alabaster flask of ointment, and standing behind him at his feet, weeping, she began to wet his feet with her tears and wiped them with	Permitted outpouring of devotion

Reference	Content	Quality
	the hair of her head and kissed his feet and anointed them with the ointment.	
Luke 7:47–48	"Therefore I tell you, her sins, which are many, are forgiven—for she loved much. But he who is forgiven little, loves little." And he said to her, "Your sins are forgiven."	Forgave women
Luke 8:2	And also some women who had been healed of evil spirits and infirmities: Mary, called Magdalene, from whom seven demons had gone out.	Cast out evil from women
Luke 10:38	Now as they [Jesus and his disciples] went on their way, Jesus entered a village. And a woman named Martha welcomed him into her house.	Accepted women's hospitality
Luke 10:39	And she had a sister called Mary, who sat at the Lord's feet and listened to his teaching.	Taught women
Luke 10:42	"But one thing is necessary. Mary has chosen the good portion, which will not be taken away from her.	Commended women's desire to learn
Luke 11:27–28	As he [Jesus] said these things, a woman in the crowd raised her voice and said to him, "Blessed is the womb that bore you, and the breasts at which you nursed!" But he said, "Blessed rather are those who hear the word of God and keep it."	Blessed women's desire to follow His word
Luke 13:12	When Jesus saw her, he called her over and said to her, "Woman, you are freed from your disability."	Healed women
Luke 23:55	The women who had come with him [Jesus] from Galilee followed and saw the tomb and how his body was laid.	Women chosen as witnesses of his burial
Luke 24:10	Now it was Mary Magdalene and Joanna and Mary the mother of James and the other women with them who told these things to the apostles.	Women chosen as evangelists

Reference	Content	Quality
John 4:7	There came a woman of Samaria to draw water. Jesus said to her, "Give me a drink."	Spoke to women directly
John 8:10–11	Jesus stood up and said to her, "Woman, where are they? Has no one condemned you?" She said, "No one, Lord." And Jesus said, "Neither do I condemn you; go, and from now on sin no more."	Pardoned women and showed them mercy
John 19:25	But standing by the cross of Jesus were his mother and his mother's sister, Mary the wife of Clopas, and Mary Magdalene.	Women chosen as steadfast witnesses of his crucifixion
John 19:26	When Jesus saw his mother and the disciple whom he loved standing nearby, he said to his mother, "Woman, behold your son!"	Cared for women
John 20:16	Jesus said to her, "Mary." She turned and said to him in Aramaic, "Rabboni!" (which means Teacher).	Women chosen as witnesses of his resurrection
John 20:18	Mary Magdalene went and announced to the disciples, "I have seen the Lord"—and that he had said these things to her.	Women chosen as evangelists of his good news

Notice that Jesus put Himself *willingly under the authority* of both of His earthly parents—His adoptive father, Joseph, and chosen mother, Mary—as He matured. As the divine Son of Yahweh, He was for all eternity joyously under the authority of His Heavenly Father, and He was pleased to demonstrate this great truth on earth through humble submission to His earthly parents.

In His ministry, Jesus spoke *directly to* women. This may not seem very profound to those of us living in the twenty-first century, but it is *amazing* in the culture of the Middle East in the first century. Social custom simply did not permit such a thing—further demonstrating how estranged gender relationships had become by this time in history. As we have already seen, free and direct social interaction between men and women is still tightly restricted in many Islamic countries today, primarily due to the concern over their inability to interact in a chaste and honorable way. For Jesus, this was never an issue.

Jesus stepped out of human convention and displayed His divine nature in an even more dramatic way. He not only spoke to women, but He *conversed at length* with them. He showered them with intense and extraordinary compassion. He healed them and those for whom they petitioned. He defended, pardoned, and honored women. He accepted their ministrations, hospitality, and support. He engaged them in theological debates and actively instructed them in the deep things of God.

And He did all of this perfectly and righteously. His interactions with them were not tainted with lust or perversion. The women He encountered were not shrouded or kept hidden from Him. By His example, He called upon all men to exhibit personal self-control. It should not be necessary for women to be hidden, shrouded, or barricaded from men to protect them from being harassed. Men should know how to behave themselves and treat women honorably and righteously in all circumstances. They should be able to be trusted:

> And what is clear from Matthew 5:28f [where Jesus defined "lust" as spiritual adultery] is that Jesus Christ means to rescue women from this attack on their personhood. Men who follow Jesus guard their eyes for the good of women and for the glory of God.[1]

MODESTY AND ELEVATION

Both women and men should still strive to be modest and to avoid exhibitionism. Biblical Christians agree with our Muslim neighbors that the human body is dreadfully exploited in many ways by contemporary culture on both sides of the globe. The echo of the fall is that we all realize the need to cover ourselves. An identifiable standard of decency exists to which most men and women subscribe, regardless of culture. We agree that "private parts" of our bodies should be covered, and we should not draw attention to them through any kind of visual "targeting." To achieve basic modesty in dress for both men and women, many kinds of clothing are acceptable, depending upon weather conditions and climate, local custom, and personal need. Beyond the basics, personal attire cannot and should not be legislated.

Jesus elevated women from being regarded solely as "wombs" or "vessels." Note particularly the passage from Luke 11 in table 6. Mary's value as a human being did not rest with her biological function. Rather, Jesus drew attention to and commended her willingness to yield her will to Yahweh's purpose and plan.

He taught that women are co-heirs of the kingdom of God. The full story of the woman he healed is in the book of Luke 13:10–17:

> Now he was teaching in one of the synagogues on the Sabbath. And there was a woman who had had a disabling spirit for eighteen years. She was bent over and could not fully straighten herself. When Jesus saw her, he called her over and said to her, "Woman, you are freed from your disability." And he laid his hands on her, and immediately she was made straight, and she glorified God. But the ruler of the synagogue, indignant because Jesus had healed on the Sabbath, said to the people, "There are six days in which work ought to be done. Come on those days and be healed, and not on the Sabbath day." Then the Lord answered him, "You hypocrites! Does not each of you on the Sabbath untie his ox or his donkey from the manger and lead it away to water it? And ought not this woman, a *daughter of Abraham* whom Satan bound for eighteen years, be loosed from this bond on the Sabbath day?" As he said these things, all his adversaries were put to shame, and all the people rejoiced at all the glorious things that were done by him.

Compassion upon this "daughter of Abraham" was far more important than an arbitrary and burdensome rule imposed by fallible men.

> And so the message of Jesus to the synagogue leaders was a message not only about their Sabbath keeping, and not only about their hypocrisy, but also about how men and women ought to relate to each other as fellow heirs of God's promises. He was saying to men in the synagogue then, and he is saying to men in the church today, "The believing women in your midst are heirs of the promises of God. They too are the meek who will inherit the earth" (Matthew 5:5). "They too are the righteous who will shine like the sun in the kingdom of their Father" (Matthew 13:43).[2]

And to top it all off, He made His first appearance in His resurrected body to a *woman*! He entrusted Mary Magdelene, a forgiven sinner, to be the first evangelist and preacher of the most profound good news of the universe! *Jesus—crucified, dead, and buried—is alive!*

Many women were numbered among the early Christians. Women assisted Jesus' ministry and suffered equally under persecution by both secular and religious authorities.

TABLE 7: MORE WOMEN IN THE NEW TESTAMENT

Reference	Content	Quality
Acts 2:18	"Even on my male servants and female servants in those days I will pour out my Spirit, and they shall prophesy." (quoting from Joel 2:28–29)	Spirit-filled, gifted with prophecy
Acts 5:14	And more than ever believers were added to the Lord, multitudes of both men and women.	Believing

Reference	Content	Quality
Acts 8:3	But Saul was ravaging the church, and entering house after house, he dragged off men and women and committed them to prison.	Imprisoned for faith
Acts 8:12	But when they believed Philip as he preached good news about the kingdom of God and the name of Jesus Christ, they were baptized, both men and women.	Baptized
Acts 9:2	And asked him for letters to the synagogues at Damascus, so that if he found any belonging to the Way, men or women, he might bring them bound to Jerusalem.	Persecuted for faith
Acts 16:14	One who heard us was a woman named Lydia, from the city of Thyatira, a seller of purple goods, who was a worshiper of God. The Lord opened her heart to pay attention to what was said by Paul.	Worshippers of God, open-hearted, attentive to Word
Acts 17:12	Many of them therefore believed, with not a few Greek women of high standing as well as men.	Prominent in society
Acts 17:34	But some men joined him and believed, among whom also were Dionysius the Areopagite and a woman named Damaris and others with them.	Named by name
Acts 18:26	He began to speak boldly in the synagogue, but when Priscilla and Aquila heard him, they took him and explained to him the way of God more accurately.	Able to teach others
Acts 22:4	I persecuted this Way to the death, binding and delivering to prison both men and women.	Bound for faith
Romans 16:12	Greet those workers in the Lord, Tryphaena and Tryphosa. Greet the beloved Persis, who has worked hard in the Lord.	Hard-working

Reference	Content	Quality
1 Corinthians 14:33–35	For God is not a God of confusion but of peace. As in all the churches of the saints, the women should keep silent in the churches. For they are not permitted to speak, but should be in submission, as the Law also says. If there is anything they desire to learn, let them ask their husbands at home. For it is shameful for a woman to speak in church.	Submit in peace
1 Timothy 2:8–12	I desire then that in every place the men should pray, lifting holy hands without anger or quarreling; likewise also that women should adorn themselves in respectable apparel, with modesty and self-control, not with braided hair and gold or pearls or costly attire, but with what is proper for women who profess godliness—with good works. Let a woman learn quietly with all submissiveness. I do not permit a woman to teach or to exercise authority over a man; rather, she is to remain quiet.	Respectable, modest, self-controlled, godly, quiet spirit

Jesus' example of loving leadership and tender regard for women, planted in the hearts of believing men through Yahweh's saving grace, transformed gender relationships within the body of believers.

SERVANT LEADERSHIP AND HONORABLE SUBMISSION

Leadership in the body of Christian believers is *servant leadership* to all the members of the congregation. It is like the original leadership of Adam before the fall, subordinated only to God Himself. Therefore, it is the responsibility of *men* within the body of believers, following the original pattern of complementarity. It is an awesome and humbling responsibility. These servant-leaders may conceivably be called upon to handle matters that are dangerous, psychologically difficult, or sexually volatile. Both men and women are called to submit to this kind of godly leadership with an attitude of peacefulness and quietude. Women are especially cautioned because Satan knows of their vulnerability in this area.

What Paul the apostle addresses in his letters to the Corinthians and to Timothy is a woman's forthright speaking out during worship. This includes distracting others, disrupting the reverence of the worshippers, attempting to usurp authority, or causing dissension in the body of believers. These passages come within the broader context of submission to authority and maintenance of order in worship. What this means is that silence, reverence, and respectful devotion should be evident in the entire body of believers—as an attitude of their hearts always.

> So what sort of quietness does Paul have in mind? It's the kind of quietness that respects and honors the leadership of the men God has called to oversee the church. Verse 11 says that the quietness is "in all submissiveness," and verse 12 says the quietness is the opposite of "authority over men," and so the point is not whether a woman says nothing, but whether she is submissive and whether she supports the authority of the men God has called to oversee the church. Quietness means not speaking in a way that compromises that authority.[3]

Biblical Christians, both men and women, are free to respond with prayer and praise during worship, provided they are not exhibitionistic or insincere. Before and after the formal worship time, they are free to greet one another, mingle socially, take counsel together, and enjoy refreshment side-by-side. But none of this should be done in a way which compromises the worshipful atmosphere of the congregation, the adherence or fellowship of the family of faith, or the authority of the church's leaders.

MARRIAGE BETWEEN CHRISTIAN BELIEVERS

Biblical complementarity has been graciously re-bestowed upon Christian marriages, not perfectly, but in a pattern we can recognize. The loving headship of man with the willing and delighted partnership of woman is reaffirmed and strengthened through the power of the Holy Spirit.

TABLE 8: MARRIAGE AMONG BELIEVERS

Reference	Content	Quality
Matthew 19:3–8	And Pharisees came up to him and tested him by asking, "Is it lawful to divorce one's wife for any cause?" He answered, "Have you not read that he who created them from the beginning made them male and female, and said, 'Therefore a man shall leave his father and his mother and hold fast to his wife, and they shall become one flesh'? So they are no longer two but one flesh. What therefore God has joined together, let not man separate." They said to him, "Why then did Moses command one to give a certificate of divorce and to send her away?" He said to them, "Because of your hardness of heart Moses allowed you to divorce your wives, but from the beginning it was not so."	Lifelong
1 Corinthians 7:2–4	But because of the temptation to sexual immorality, each man should have his own wife and each woman her own husband. The husband should give to his wife her conjugal rights, and likewise the wife to her husband. For the wife does not have authority over her own body, but the husband does. Likewise the husband does not have authority over his own body, but the wife does.	Exclusivity and shared authority over sexual matters

Reference	Content	Quality
1 Corinthians 7:10–11	To the married I give this charge (not I, but the Lord): the wife should not separate from her husband (but if she does, she should remain unmarried or else be reconciled to her husband), and the husband should not divorce his wife.	Inseparable
1 Corinthians 7:14	For the unbelieving husband is made holy because of his wife, and the unbelieving wife is made holy because of her husband. . . .	Holy
1 Corinthians 7:28	But if you do marry, you have not sinned, and if a betrothed woman marries, she has not sinned. Yet those who marry will have worldly troubles, and I would spare you that.	Not necessary for salvation
1 Corinthians 7:34	And the unmarried or betrothed woman is anxious about the things of the Lord, how to be holy in body and spirit. But the married woman is anxious about worldly things, how to please her husband.	Not necessary for salvation
1 Corinthians 11:3	But I want you to understand that the head of every man is Christ, the head of a wife is her husband, and the head of Christ is God.	Loving headship of husband in pattern of Jesus
1 Corinthians 11:12	For as woman was made from man, so man is now born of woman. And all things are from God.	Both under God
2 Corinthians 11:2	I feel a divine jealousy for you, for I betrothed you to one husband [Yahweh], to present you as a pure virgin to Christ.	Pure
1 Corinthians 14:35	If there is anything they desire to learn, let them ask their husbands at home. For it is shameful for a woman to speak in church.	Wife as student, quiet spirit
Colossians 3:18–19	Wives, submit to your husbands, as is fitting in the Lord. Husbands, love your wives, and do not be harsh with them.	Submissive and loving

Reference	Content	Quality
1 Timothy 3:1–5	The saying is trustworthy: If anyone aspires to the office of overseer, he desires a noble task. Therefore an overseer must be above reproach, the husband of one wife, sober-minded, self-controlled, respectable, hospitable, able to teach, not a drunkard, not violent but gentle, not quarrelsome, not a lover of money. He must manage his own household well, with all dignity keeping his children submissive, for if someone does not know how to manage his own household, how will he care for God's church?	Leaders should have one wife only and a well-managed household
Titus 1:6–9	If anyone is above reproach, the husband of one wife, and his children are believers and not open to the charge of debauchery or insubordination. For an overseer, as God's steward, must be above reproach. He must not be arrogant or quick-tempered or a drunkard or violent or greedy for gain, but hospitable, a lover of good, self-controlled, upright, holy, and disciplined. He must hold firm to the trustworthy word as taught, so that he may be able to give instruction in sound doctrine and also to rebuke those who contradict it.	Leaders' marriages and families are examples
Titus 2:3–5	Older women likewise are to be reverent in behavior, not slanderers or slaves to much wine. They are to teach what is good, and so train the young women to love their husbands and children, to be self-controlled, pure, working at home, kind, and submissive to their own husbands, that the word of God may not be reviled.	Loving and submissive

Men and Women in Biblical Christianity

Reference	Content	Quality
1 Peter 3:1–7	Likewise, wives, be subject to your own husbands, so that even if some do not obey the word, they may be won without a word by the conduct of their wives—when they see your respectful and pure conduct. Do not let your adorning be external—the braiding of hair, the wearing of gold, or the putting on of clothing—but let your adorning be the hidden person of the heart with the imperishable beauty of a gentle and quiet spirit, which in God's sight is very precious. For this is how the holy women who hoped in God used to adorn themselves, by submitting to their husbands, as Sarah obeyed Abraham, calling him lord. And you are her children, if you do good and do not fear anything that is frightening. Likewise, husbands, live with your wives in an understanding way, showing honor to the woman as the weaker vessel, since they are heirs with you of the grace of life, so that your prayers may not be hindered.	Submissive, honorable, co-heirs

These passages are all helpful, but the deepest spiritual discussion on marriage in the New Testament is given in Ephesians 5:21–33:

> Wives, submit to your own husbands, as to the Lord. For the husband is the head of the wife even as Christ is the head of the church, his body, and is himself its Savior. Now as the church submits to Christ, so also wives should submit in everything to their husbands.
>
> Husbands, love your wives, as Christ loved the church and gave himself up for her, that he might sanctify her, having cleansed her by the washing of water with the word,

so that he might present the church to himself in splendor, without spot or wrinkle or any such thing, that she might be holy and without blemish. In the same way husbands should love their wives as their own bodies. He who loves his wife loves himself. For no one ever hated his own flesh, but nourishes and cherishes it, just as Christ does the church, because we are members of his body.

"Therefore a man shall leave his father and mother and hold fast to his wife, and the two shall become one flesh." *This mystery is profound, and I am saying that it refers to Christ and the church.* However, let each one of you love his wife as himself, and let the wife see that she respects her husband.

LOVE AND HONOR

Believers in Christ willingly acknowledge and affirm the original creation model with regard to man's headship within the marriage covenant. This headship is *not* sovereign authority, for that is God's alone. It is not autocratic control, for that is tyranny. It is not the assertion of male rights or powers over women, for that is despotism.

Christian headship is generous and loving leadership, in the model of Christ himself. It is the husband's willingness, responsibility, and dedication to *lay down his life for his wife.*

> If you want to understand God's meaning for marriage you have to grasp that we are dealing with a copy and an original, a metaphor and a reality, a parable and a truth. And the original, the reality, the truth is God's marriage to his people, or Christ's marriage to the church. While the copy, the metaphor, the parable is a husband's marriage to his wife.[4]

Christian men and women no longer face off against one another in enmity. Now they face God together. It becomes a great blessing once again for a woman to be in submission to a man who reflects God's love toward her:

> When a man senses a primary God-given responsibility for the spiritual life of the family, gathering the family for devotions, taking them to church, calling for prayer at meals—when he senses a primary God-given responsibility for the discipline and education of the children, the stewardship of money, the provision of food, the safety of the home, the healing of discord, that special sense of responsibility is not authoritarian or autocratic or domineering or bossy or oppressive or abusive. It is simply servant-leadership. And I have never met a wife who is sorry she is married to a man like that. Because when God designs a thing (like marriage) he designs it for his glory and our good.[5]
>
> Submission refers to a wife's divine calling to honor and affirm her husband's leadership and help carry it through according to her gifts. It is not an absolute surrender of her will. Rather, we speak of her *disposition to yield* to her husband's guidance and her *inclination* to follow his leadership. Christ is her absolute authority, not the husband. She submits "out of reverence for Christ" (Ephesians 5:21). The supreme authority of Christ qualifies the authority of her husband. She should never follow her husband into sin. Nevertheless, even when she may have to stand with Christ against the sinful will of her husband (e.g., 1 Peter 3:1, where she does not yield to her husband's unbelief), she can still have a *spirit* of submission—a *disposition* to yield. She can show by her attitude and behavior that she does not like resisting his will and that she longs for him to forsake sin and lead in righteousness so that her disposition to honor him as head can again produce harmony.[6]

GUIDELINES FOR PROPER SUBMISSION

Biblical Christianity also affirms that *a Christian woman is not called to be submissive in all ways to all men at all times.* A woman is not to submit sexually or emotionally to any man other than her own husband. A woman is not to submit to any ungodly or decadent demands or to any practices and behaviors that are clearly contrary to Scripture, even if her husband makes them (a situation she should never have to face if her husband is a true Biblical Christian). A woman is not to submit her mature judgment to the whims of male children—hers or anyone else's.

There may be times when a Christian woman is called upon to assume temporary or limited leadership. Her husband may delegate certain decisions to her by mutual agreement or in the event of his absence, illness, or other inability to lead. She might be called upon to provide counsel to men who may need greater understanding of a topic about which she may have more training or experience. She might need to correct a young man or admonish an old man, if the behavior of either is clearly contrary to basic Biblical guidelines.

> All leadership falls somewhere on the scale between very impersonal (little personal contact) and very personal (a lot of personal contact). . . . To the degree that a woman's leadership of man is personal it needs to be non-directive. And to the degree that it is directive, it needs to be impersonal. To the degree that a woman consistently offers directive, personal leadership to a man, to that degree will his God-given manhood—his sense of responsibility in the relationship—be compromised. What's at stake every time a man and a woman relate to each other is not merely competence (that is very naïve), but also whether God-given manhood and womanhood are affirmed in the dynamics of the relationship.[7]

What exactly does this mean? It means that a woman may demonstrate a lot of leadership over men *at a distance.* Examples of this may be a female member of a legislative body, a female lecturer at a university, or a female head physician in a hospital. In such situations, she may have men under her authority. These scenarios bring with them certain dangers in our fallen world and should not be assumed without a great deal of counsel and support, especially from others in the community of faith. Male-female relationships under these conditions must remain business-like and above reproach.

A woman *may* be called upon in certain circumstances to demonstrate leadership among men in a more personal way. These are generally within the family: as an in-law, the parent of a grown son, or perhaps the trusted advisor of a male relative. In this case, her authority is most effective when it is non-directive. For this, we have the wonderful example of Abigail in 1 Samuel 25:23-35. Rather than shame her husband or call attention to his folly, she graciously covered his rudeness with her own gentle hospitality.

A Biblical Christian woman is first and foremost a *Christian*, which means that she has been called into a personal relationship with Jesus Christ. Her heart, mind, soul, and strength are all yielded to Jesus, Who infuses her with His Spirit and enables her by His redeeming grace to fulfill her calling.

She may remain single; there is no shame, incompleteness, or inadequacy in being unmarried. Within Biblical Christian fellowships, God sometimes calls specific men or women into extended periods or perhaps entire lives of singleness to fulfill His purposes (1 Corinthians 7). Marriage is not mandatory, nor is singleness looked down upon:

> The healing which Jesus brings to male and female created in God's image is not dependent on marriage. In fact Paul's experience as a single man (and the model of Jesus as a single man) taught him that there is a kind of single-minded devotion to the Lord possible to the single man or woman that is not usually the portion of married saints.[8]

But if she is married, helping her husband is a major part of her calling. This takes different forms for different families, but one thing is certain: Christian couples serve the Lord together as a team in covenant.

Not quite the garden, but Biblical Christianity affirms that through Jesus the "Way" is open once again. . . .

Is Islam the Answer?

The foundational, original text documents of Islam will not change. The schools of Islamic thought, intent on adhering to the strictest interpretations of both the Noble Qur'an and the Hadith, are frozen in time through the classical rulings of the past. The frequently-heard call in Arab countries that "Islam Is the Answer" is a call back to a mythical "golden age of Islam," which is romanticized as the era of pure, real, and true Islam.

But Islam was never pure or real or true at all. And a call to it is a call to bondage for women.

FUNDAMENTALIST ISLAM = ORTHODOX ISLAM

Islamic fundamentalist groups are lead by men who are well educated in the doctrines of orthodox Islam. Many hold degrees from Islamic universities or Qur'anic schools. Most are considered "clerics" and are often addressed with titles such as "ayatollah," "imam," or "mullah." Contrary to the protests of contemporary Muslim apologists, especially those in the West, the fundamental teachings of Islam these leaders present is entirely accurate.

In Afghanistan, the fundamentalist group was the Taliban—a word that means "students." Members of the Taliban were all disciples of classical Islam, knew the Noble Qur'an *by heart*, and studied the Hadith and the various schools of Islamic law meticulously. The kind of government the Taliban instituted is a prime example of what fundamentalist ("original text") Islam's perfect world would be like.

Without exception, countries overtaken by fundamental Islamic power-groups like the Taliban show extreme deterioration in all parameters of social, political, and religious life for women. Leila Ahmed, in her impressive book titled *Women and Gender in Islam*, notes:

> States in which Islamic groups have recently seized power and reinstituted Islamic laws have thus far invariably enacted laws imposing severe new restrictions on women and sometimes also laws resulting in savage injustice and inhumanity toward women.
>
> Researchers have found that in Pakistan "the vilification of women increased . . . in direct proportion to the spouting of self-righteous declarations of a new Islamic order."[1]

Ahmed is sympathetic to Islam, yet is compelled by academic honesty to enumerate examples of legislation and rhetoric directed at the subjugation of women in these societies. At the conclusion of the list, she writes:

> All the above laws and decrees, those of both Iran and Pakistan, directly reflect or are entirely compatible with Sharia views as interpreted by establishment Islam. There is every reason to believe that any government declaring itself committed to Islamization, along either Sunni or Shia lines, would introduce similar laws for women.[2]

Ahmed is incredulous that in a recent survey the majority of Egyptian women, both veiled and unveiled, were *positive* toward recent proposals that Egyptian civil law be brought into greater conformity with shari'ah law. Ahmed writes:

> It is surely extremely doubtful that either group has any idea of the extremes of control, exclusion, injustice, and indeed brutality that can be, in the present order of things, legitimately meted out to women in the name of Islam.[3]

It is not necessary or desirable in this book to describe these extreme and horrific things. Many are well known. The complete and total veiling of women in Afghanistan (wearing the burqa) is actually one of the *milder* outcomes. Others are more hidden and insidious, including the persistent practice of maliciously maiming and killing women in the name of "honor," carried out by male family members (including drowning, stoning, stabbing, and burning), female genital mutilation (claimed as a cultural practice, but endorsed within certain branches of Islam), and public beating and humiliation for women who are not dressed appropriately or who wear makeup or other such forbidden items. This book cannot contain the number of documented events of these kinds. A bibliography of resources on these topics begins on page 123. These resources are compelling and appalling reading.

MEDIA FOCUS ON WOMEN IN ISLAM

Secular resources are replete with information on women's status in Islamic countries. *Time* magazine ran a special issue titled "Lifting the Veil." Here are some excerpts:[4]

> It is hard to find a woman in Kabul now who does not remember *a beating at the hands of the Taliban.*

> As Riffat Hassan, professor of religious studies at the University of Louisville, puts it, "the way Islam has been practiced in most Muslim societies for centuries has *left millions of Muslim women with battered bodies, minds, and souls.*"

Wife beating is so prevalent in the Muslim world that social workers who assist battered women in Egypt, for example, spend much of their time trying to convince victims that their husbands' violent acts are unacceptable.

Sexual anxiety lies at the heart of many Islamic strictures on women.

Wives in Islamic societies face great difficulty in suing for divorce, but *husbands can be released from their vows virtually on demand*, in some places merely by saying "I divorce you" three times.

In Iran the legal age for marriage is nine for girls, 14 for boys. The law has occasionally been exploited by pedophiles, who marry poor young girls from the provinces, use and then abandon them.

Recently a fundamentalist group in the Indian province of Kashmir demanded that women start wearing veils. When the call was ignored, *hooligans threw acid in the faces of uncovered women.*

Today the only legal evidence of a Saudi woman's existence is in the appearance of her name on her husband's card.

Asked about the controversial Koranic sura 4:34—with its *sanction of spousal punishment*, including beating, for "insubordination"—Kareem [Irfan], who is chairman of the Islamic Organizations of Greater Chicago, is bemused. *"It's amazing how many men know this quote from the Koran—if they know nothing else in it,"* he says.

Additional quotations could go on and on, but the point has been made.

Omid Zareian, in a report entitled "Women as Seen in Islam," defines the process of stoning females who are convicted of adultery in Iran:

> "In the punishment of stoning to death, the stones should not be too large so that the person dies on being hit by one or two of them; they should not be so small either that they could not be defined as stones" (Law of Hodoud and Qesas. Article 119. Majlis [parliament] 1999). This demonstrates the cruelty and the other articles of the Hodoud and Qesas law [of Iran] shocks any concerned human being.[5]

In "Lifting the Veil on Sex Slavery" in *Time*, we read:

> Now it is clear from the testimony of witnesses and officials of the new government [of Afghanistan] that the *ruling clerics* systematically abducted women from the Tajik, Uzbek, Hazara and other ethnic minorities they defeated. Stolen women were a reward for victorious battle.[6]

We have already read how the Noble Qur'an and the Hadith sanction the taking of females from conquered populations. By orthodox Islamic logic, if a practice was permitted in the past, it should be permitted in the present and be continued in the future. Reinterpretation or reformation of the original documents, teachings, and legal rulings is difficult, if not impossible. Islam does not "change its mind."

INTERNET RESOURCES PROMOTING RESTRICTIONS ON WOMEN UNDER ISLAM ABOUND

Muslim apologetics are readily found on the web on all kinds of topics of special interest to Muslim women. Muslim scholars are quoted at length, and commentators offer advice on such issues as proper veiling and suitable Islamic dress, prayer, polygamy, wife beating, etc.

Here are brief samples of the cyber-discourse found on the Internet in the United States for and about women under Islam. We strongly invite readers to look up these sources online and read them in their entirety.

> The veil which she must put on is one that can save her soul from weakness, her mind from indulgence, her eyes from lustful looks, and her personality from demoralization.[7]

> Your body is on display in the market of Shaitaan [Satan] seducing the hearts of men. The hairstyles, the tight clothing showing every detail of your figure, the short dresses showing off your legs and feet, the showy, decorative and fragrant clothing all *angers the Merciful and pleases the Shaitaan*. Every day that passes while you are in this condition, *distances you further from Allah and brings you closer to Shaitaan. Each day curses and anger are directed toward you from the heavens until you repent.* Every day brings you closer to the grave and the Angel of Death is ready to capture your soul.[8]

Islam's answer to the inability and unwillingness of Muslim men to control their eyes is to cover women in a variety of creative ways. Some are actually dangerous to their health and safety. But the practice of covering women does not address the real heart of the matter.

The heart of the matter is *spiritual*. Both men and women must be changed from the *inside* in order to regard and respond to one another with self-control and modesty. External clothing will never be sufficient for this purpose. It wasn't in the original garden, and it won't be today.

COMMON RULES FOR MUSLIM WOMEN

A woman who is *in her monthly cycle* cannot:
1. Perform the five prescribed prayers (Salat al Fard) (prayers missed due to menstruation do not have to be made up)

2. Touch the Qur'an,
3. Make ta'waf around the Kaba,
4. Fast *(Days of fasting missed during Ramadan may be made up within the next lunar year)*
5. Engage in sexual intercourse with her husband (kissing, hugging, and other intimate touching outside of the genital area is okay).
6. *It is better for her not to be in the musallah* (area where prayers are performed) in the masjid or Islamic centre.[9]

The *Los Angeles Times* recently reported that a court in Cairo, Egypt, overturned a 1996 government ban on health workers carrying out female circumcision. The ruling had been sought by eight *Islamic scholars* and doctors who argued that the *ban was in violation of religious beliefs* and interfered with physician's prerogatives to perform medical duties. "For practical purposes, the ban will remain in effect until a final verdict is reached in the higher courts. In addition, *most girls undergo the operation at home at the hands of unlicensed midwives or barbers who use razor blades to cut off part or all the labia and clitoris.* In some cases, they also sew closed the vaginal opening until the child is old enough to be married," the report said. A recent survey of about 15000 women between 15 and 49 in urban and rural areas revealed that 97% had undergone the operation. Those in favor of circumcision argue that uncircumcised girls will be considered loose or they believe that circumcision helps cleanliness.[10]

It is perfectly Islamic to hold meetings of men and women inside the Masjid, whether for prayers or for any other Islamic purpose, without separating them with a curtain, partition or wall. It is, however, very important that Muslim women come to public gatherings wearing proper Islamic dress. *It is haram [shameful] for a Muslim woman to attend a public gathering without a full Islamic dress.* She must cover her hair and neck with a scarf which should also go over her bosom. Her dress should be modest and loose enough in order not to reveal the shape of her body. . . .

If there is a concern that the lines of men and women will mix inside the Masjid, then there is no harm in putting a lower barrier, only to demarcate the separate area for women. But women should not be put in a totally separate room in the Masjid unless there is a shortage of space and *no other proper arrangement can be done for them.*[11]

And among those mosques that do let women in, I'm sorry to say that most of the ones I have seen relegate the women to an inferior status. They banish them to basement rooms or other segregated spaces. Too often the second-class spaces allotted to the women are poorly maintained, uncomfortable, cramped, filthy, or otherwise substandard, while the men reserve the best areas for their exclusive use. *This kind of treatment makes the preaching about women's status being equal in Islam sound awfully hollow.* Too many places don't allow women any chance to speak and be heard, let alone have any say in the way the mosque is run.[12]

Therefore, when a Muslim woman wants to go to work abroad, she must be accompanied by her husband or a close relative whom she may not marry.[13]

As for the presence of many men and women in a social gathering or in a lecture hall or a meeting hall this is permissible in Islam, provided that women should wear proper Islamic dress which *covers their heads and all their bodies with the exception of their faces and the lower part of their hands.*[14]

We advise women not to look at *mahram* [forbidden] men. *It is best for the woman if she is not seen by the men* and she does not see them. There is no difference on this point between a battlefield or a sports field. *A woman is weak and can easily be swayed.* Many times, a woman looks at a movie or picture of a young man and her emotions and desires are excited. This expose[s] her to temptation. Being away from the causes of temptation is always the safest approach.[15]

Since no clear prohibition is made, then we cannot say that for a man to shake hands with a woman is forbidden, but *refraining from it* is certainly preferable.[16]

In some communities, social contact between men and women who are not related is completely forbidden, thus resulting in segregated schools, businesses, government offices, and the virtual exclusion of women from positions of power or control. The domination and oppression of women has resulted from restrictions on social interactions *enabling the leadership in governments to deny basic human rights* and use Islam to support their position. In general, many Muslims have adopted the justification for such separation, inspired by the fear that allowing social contact will encourage and undoubtedly lead to illicit sexual behavior.[17]

Although both men and women are subject to such mistreatment [sexual harassment], it is ultimately much more an *exercise of male power* rooted deep in the economic and social position and authority they enjoy in the home, workplace and society.[18]

Gender relations in Pakistan rest on two basic perceptions: that *women are subordinate to men, and that a man's honor resides in the actions of the women of his family.* Thus, as in other orthodox Muslim societies, women are responsible for maintaining the family honor. To ensure that they do not dishonor their families, society limits women's mobility, places restrictions on their behavior and activities, and permits them only limited contact with the opposite sex. Space is allocated to and used differently by men and women. For their protection and respectability, women have traditionally been expected to live under the constraints of purdah (purdah is Persian for curtain), most obvious in veiling. By separating women from the activities of men, both physically and symbolically, purdah creates differentiated male and female spheres. *Most women spend the major part of their lives physically within their homes and courtyards* and go out only for serious and approved reasons.[19]

There are several Islamic attitudes apparent in the preceding excerpts:

- Menstruation is a dirty thing, preventing women from full participation in the spiritual life of the ummah (community of believers). This causes a "deficiency in religion" for her, which in practicality can never be overcome.
- Children take precedence over women during corporate prayer, an attitude made clear by their preferential placement within the mosque.
- Women must obey conventions of dress and/or physical separation to stay socially sequestered from contact with men. Men continue to enjoy complete freedom in these areas.
- Men are dominant in Islamic society and are free to exercise their power over women in a variety of ways without social sanction or loss of honor. In fact, if he does not control women, he is dishonored and shamed.

THE RATIONALE FOR POLYGAMY

The system of polygamy according to Islamic Law is a moral, human system. It is moral because it does not allow man to have intercourse with any woman he wishes, at any time he likes. He is not allowed to have intercourse with more than three women in addition to his (first) wife, and he cannot do that secretly, but must proceed with a contract and announce it, even among a limited audience. The people *in charge of the woman* should know about this lawful intercourse and agree to it or *at least should not object to it*. It should be registered—according to the modern system—in a specialised court for marriage contracts. *It is desirable to have a special dinner for the occasion in which the man invites his friends*. Dufoof (hand drums) may be played to *express utmost joy and hospitality*.[20]

The institute of polygamy is always looked down upon as an injustice to women folks. Is it really so? On the contrary consider the following salient features, which *distinctly work in favor of women*.

1. Polygamy gives an opportunity to the woman to choose a life partner who has already *proven himself as a good husband*, thereby reducing the matrimonial risks.
2. It extends practical security to a woman against loosing [losing] her husband (and everything else with him) to *some other better-qualified woman*, as it happens in case of monogamy.
3. It *safeguards her husband* from possible adultery and it's disastrous ill effects.
4. It gives a possible way out to a career-minded woman to pursue her career by having a *female friend* & husband to share family responsibilities.
5. It keeps a *check on men from flirting* with young girls and not marrying them on the pretext of their existing marriages.[21]

There is no doubt that the woman who has *one-half of a husband or one-third or one-fourth* is better off than the one who has no husband at all.[22]

The above excerpts crush the heart of Biblical Christians. Polygamy sanctions man's lust. Islam disregards a woman's God-given need to feel exclusively loved and treasured. Polygamy does not protect women—it violates their trust. The "logic" employed to help Muslim women accept this is twisted and frightening. It didn't work in Muhammad's household, and it won't work today.

THE DISCIPLINING AND DIVORCE OF A WIFE

Contrary to Christianity, *Islam does not regard marriages as "made in heaven" or "till death do us part."* They are contracts, with conditions. If either side breaks the conditions, divorce is not only allowed, but usually expected.[23]

The controversy with divorce lies in the idea that *men seem to have absolute power in divorce.* The way the scholars in the past have interpreted this is that if the man initiates the divorce, then the reconciliation step for appointing an arbiter from both sides is omitted.[24]

What should one make of the verse in the Koran that allows a man to punish his wife physically? There are important provisos: he may do so only *if her ill-will is wrecking the marriage*—but then only after he has exhausted all attempts at verbal communication and tried sleeping in a separate bed.[25]

The first three [methods for disciplining a wife] are to be tried first. If they fail, then the help of the families should be sought. It has to be noted, in the light of the above verses, that *beating the rebellious wife is a temporary measure*, that is resorted to as third in line in cases of extreme necessity, in hopes that it might remedy the *wrongdoing of the wife.* If it does, the husband is not allowed by any means to continue any annoyance to the wife as explicitly mentioned in the verse. If it does not, the husband is still not allowed to use this measure any longer and the final avenue of the family-assisted reconciliation has to be explored. The Arabic word "dharb" is usually translated as "beating" which is a much too hard definition for it. "Dharb" is a *slight strike or slap.*[26]

Some husbands get *upset when their wives refuse to do this or that around the house.* This has subjected many wives to physical mistreatment.[27]

As Muslims we must acknowledge that in some cases, *imams and community leaders are actually perpetrating violence on their families.* In such cases, interventions must be sensibly planned without informing or consulting these individuals. With a goal to diffuse the situation quickly, the intervention team will ideally include at least one individual which the abuser respects as his equal (i.e., a religious scholar or another imam).[28]

An Italian charity, Smile Again, is teaming up with Depilex beauty salons from September to provide reconstructive plastic surgery for the victims of acid and kerosene attacks. Reporting of such attacks on women is on the increase in Pakistan.
    The charity already works in Bangladesh and India where *this form of violence against women is common.*[29]

Indeed, the legal system and law enforcement agencies including police officers and prison guards, have been implicated in the perpetuation of the problem [of honor killings] by their *willful lenience towards men who have carried out an assault in the name of "honor" and by their abuse and denigration of women who stand accused.*[30]

The words used to describe punishable behavior, determined solely by her husband, are subjective judgment words, such as ill-will, rebellious, and wrongdoing.[31]
    Muslims are on a slippery slope here. A "slight strike or slap" is just the first step on a continuum of physical violence that easily leads to violent assault or murder in the name of "honor." The truth of this is documented over and over again in Islamic societies.

WOMEN'S SALVATION IN ISLAM

Muslim women view the teachings of Islam as their best friend and supporter. The prescriptions that are found in the Quran and in the example of the Prophet Muhammad, salallahu alehi wasallam, are *regarded as the ideal to which contemporary women wish to return.*[32]

The thought and practice of Muslims have come lately to misrepresent most of the doctrinal and normative teachings of Islam on female affairs. The female is hardly ever religiously addressed except through *the mediation of the male and as an addendum to him.* In the fallen society of Muslims, women have little freedom to marry the person she likes, or to separate from a husband she loathes. Nor is she, as wife, entitled to full consultation and gracious companionship by her husband. In many cases she hardly enjoys an equal opportunity to earn and own property, or the full capacity to manage her property or to dispose thereof. *All sorts of subterfuges are employed to deny her inheritance.* Her role in private life has been reduced to that of a housewife chosen not for her personal merit, for she was denied the education or the opportunity to acquire merit, but for *the merit of her menfolk.*[33]

True success is fulfilling our roles as women and living up to Allah's expectations of us as being *mothers of steadfast Muslims.* Those are the deeds truly worth bringing to our graves and *the only deeds worthy of showing Allah on the final day.* May Allah grant us mercy. Ameen.[34]

By preventing marriage, one loses out on the benefits of marriage. I advise my brother Muslims who are the *guardians of women* and my sister Muslims not to keep from marriage due to finishing school or teaching. In fact, the woman may put a condition upon her husband that she may remain studying until she finishes her studies or she remain teaching for a year or two, given that she does not become busy with her children. There is no harm in such an act. However, a matter which needs further consideration is where the woman is continuing her studies in an area that is not truly needed. In my view, when *a woman finishes the elementary stages and has the ability to read and write*, thereby being able to benefit from her knowledge through reading the Book of Allah, its tafseer, the hadith of the Prophet (peace be upon him) and their explanation, *that is all she really needs*. Unless, of course, she is continuing her studies in an area that the people need, such as medicine and similar fields. This is also *conditional that the study not involve aspects which are forbidden, such as mixing with men* and so forth.[35]

What can we do as Muslims to help? First of all, we must *build true Qur'anic societies throughout the Muslim World*. Without these, we cannot establish equitable and viable accommodation for the interaction of men and women in society.[36]

The fundamental rule in Qur'anic exegesis is ensuring that the derived meaning is in conformity with the integrity of the Qur'an. When this is considered, it is seen that *all the rules mentioned to us by Allah regarding women form a social structure allowing them to live in the most comfortable and happiest way. In a society where all the moral values mentioned by Islam are practiced comprehensively, the social position of women becomes even more exalted* than in societies that we today regard as modern.[37]

Major problem areas that need to be addressed include the following:

- Family laws pertaining to marriage and divorce that reinforce the image of relationships based on a hierarchy with the rights of the husband superceding those of the wife and that prevent women from being in control of their lives.

- Violence against women which occurs in the home, community, and as a consequence of warfare which is claimed by some to be allowed by Islam when it is not.
- Abuse of certain Islamic practices that affect women negatively, such as polygamy and temporary marriage, when applied out of context and without abiding by Islamic restrictions.
- Excluding women from religious activities such as attendance in the mosque which has clearly been established as the Muslim woman's right.
- Failure to promote the importance of a woman's contribution to society beyond child-bearing.
- Failure to enable women to take advantage of rights of property ownership and inheritance outlined by Islam.
- Focusing on the behavior of women as a marker for morality in society and subjecting them to harassment, intimidation or discrimination.
- Lack of awareness of the important role of men in contributing significantly in sharing household responsibilities and child-rearing as exemplified by Prophet Muhammed.[38]

All the cruelties and heinous acts of violence, perpetrated by Muslims throughout the centuries were inspired by Qur'an and Sunnah (the example of the prophet).[39]

BACK TO THE "GOLDEN AGE" OF ISLAM . . .

What women such as Shagufta, Maha, Soraya, Fareena and Jasmin want is to return to the freedoms that Islam brought women in the 7th century and beyond, when women became prominent Islamic scholars, poets and thinkers. "We need a reformation in this global community," said Fareena. "We need to go back to the Islam of the golden age from the 7th to the 13th century." Soraya recognises that *this desire to return to the 7th century is paradoxically close to the avowed aims of the Taliban and other fundamentalist groups*, but the struggle is over interpretations of what is the true Islam, and British Muslim women are all too well aware of how fragile their position is, defending themselves against criticism from all sides—both from the westerners who accuse them of being oppressed and from the traditional Muslim cultures shocked by their independence and "Westernization."[40]

The Islamic Emirate of Afghanistan [i.e., the Taliban] is fully committed to the social, cultural and economic development of women. The government has been able to protect the honor, life and property of Afghan women.[41]

Muslim practices today often oppress women and deny them the equality and human dignity granted in the Qur'an.[42]

Islam is deeply anti-woman. Islam is the fundamental cause of the repression of Muslim women and remains the major obstacle to the evolution of their position. Islam has always considered women as creatures inferior in every way: physically, intellectually, and morally. This negative vision is divinely sanctioned in the Koran, corroborated by the *hadiths*, and perpetuated by the commentaries of the theologians, the custodians of Muslim dogma and ignorance.[43]

I have noticed in forums over and over that if Muslims call attention to systemic injustice against women in Muslim countries, they are *likely to get attacked and accused of supporting kufr* against Islam.[44]

FREEDOM FOR MUSLIM WOMEN

We feel that we, as Muslim Americans, have opportunities to openly address the challenges facing American Muslim women. As Americans we have access to a legal system that was formulated to protect the rights of those who suffer abuse. The *laws of the United States* guarantee us certain freedoms, such as the freedoms of religion and speech. We have legal avenues to fight discrimination and abuse. *We also have the ability to engage in open and honest dialogues without fear of retribution* from the government. Moreover, the women's movement in the United States has made great strides in bringing to light the abuses suffered by women and offering avenues of redress.[45]

It has recently dawned on me that *North America is the only place where Muslim women can exercise the full range of rights and freedoms they enjoy in the original Sharî'ah.* In too many Muslim countries overseas women are kept in subjugation and even suffer violence because their sharî rights are denied. Even at the hands of the official "Islamic" authorities, which is a disgrace to the ummah. The worst violator is the Taliban regime, who oppress and beat women based on their crude tribal customs and try to pass it off as Islam. What an embarrassment to Muslims the world over. Of all Muslim countries, the one that has perhaps the best record of respecting women's Islamic rights under the Sharî'ah is Iran.[46]

The last comment is intensely revealing to any thoughtful person. This dear woman realizes that North America, with its system of civil law founded on the principles rooted in Biblical Christianity, is the *only* place where she can experience what she is deceived into expecting from Islamic "shari'ah."

What a paradox this is!

A CRY OF THE HEART

An Iranian woman wrote this about her life in her homeland:

> There is a place a mere five hours' flight from where I sit writing this book where I have a price, and that price is that of just half a man.

There is another world, a strange world where a man can kill me and escape execution unless my family pays to top up my worth to the price of a man.

If my father should die in this other world, I inherit one share to every two shares my brother gets. And if my husband dies I can expect only one-eighth of the life we built together.

There is a place, just five hours from here, where sons belong to their mother for only the first seven years of their lives.

There is a place where I am only half a witness in its courts.

There is a place where I need my father's permission to marry, no matter what my age.

There is a place where I need my husband's consent to get a passport and his agreement before I can travel.

There is a place, just five hours' flight from here, where I am but half a man.[47]

THE TRUTH ABOUT WOMEN UNDER ISLAM

So, what's the bottom line? Simply this:

Cultures which are . . .
- Founded upon and dedicated to the implementation of orthodox, fundamentalist Islam's law and teachings

- Turning out scholar after scholar from Islamic madrassahs and Muslim universities and placing them in positions of power within government and society
- Deriving their sense of identity and value from orthodox, fundamentalist Islam, and continue to study intensively

. . . are cultures that *never have been and never will be* able to provide any woman with the "full range of rights and freedoms" she imagines she should have under the "original shari'ah" of Islam.

How can this be? What she doesn't realize is that the oppression those "radical" Islamic societies implement *is* the original shari'ah, the "answer of Islam." It is all she can ever expect to experience in cultures embracing it.

Seven

A Quest of the Mind and a Cry of the Heart

The quest of the mind and the cry of every human heart is to know the truth and to feel loved and valued. The Holy Bible affirms and satisfies this need. Societies founded upon scriptural precepts extend this graciousness to their citizens. It is, indeed, a strong ideal, and draws men and women to Biblical faith from all over the world.

Although we all sin and fall far short of perfection, we are all desperate for others to accept us and for God to offer us compassion. Yet if we are perfectly honest with ourselves, we must admit that we are totally unable to be "good enough" to merit such high regard. Deep down inside, we all know that we cannot climb out of this fallen place on our own effort.

And although God has established civil government for the benefit of human society, no system of laws can bring us out of it either.

We need a deliverer, a *savior*.

Biblical Christians believe that God Himself answered this cry. And the answer is Jesus:

God created us in His image, but we have marred it almost beyond recognition and Jesus is the answer. He comes by faith, He forgives, He cleanses, and He begins a reclamation project called sanctification that will end in the glory that God intended for human beings in the first place. Therefore since we know that we were created in the image of God, our sin and corruption begs for an answer. And Jesus is the answer.[1]

He came to us in the garden and He comes to us now. He communed with us then and He communes with us now. He lived among us then and He lives within us now. He loved us then; He has not ceased to love us now. In Him there is ultimate and complete safety, acceptance, and forgiveness.

Muslims and Christians both believe that Jesus will come again. For Biblical Christians, Jesus returns as a King to reign forever and ever.[2] The Holy Bible describes Jesus' return in terms that are especially poignant to women. As a King, He will come for His "bride," those who are called by His name and have been brought under His care.

> His betrothed bride is the people of God—the people who trust him, elect from every race and nation, the church. He came the first time 2,000 years ago to die for his bride—to pay a dowry, as it were, with his own blood. And he will come a second time to marry her and take us—his church—into the gardens and the chambers of his love and joy forever.[3]

He does not desire to control His bride, or punish her, or demean her in any way. He *loves* her! See table 9.

TABLE 9: JESUS' LOVE IN THE NEW TESTAMENT

Reference	Content
John 15:13	Greater love has no one than this, that someone lays down his life for his friends.

Reference	Content
John 17:26	I made known to them your name, and I will continue to make it known, that the love with which you have loved me may be in them [believers], and I in them.
Romans 5:5	Because God's love has been poured into our hearts through the Holy Spirit who has been given to us.
Romans 5:8	But God shows his love for us in that while we were still sinners, Christ died for us.
Romans 8:39	Nor height nor depth, nor anything else in all creation, will be able to separate us from the love of God in Christ Jesus our Lord.
Romans 13:8	The one who loves another has fulfilled the law.
1 Corinthians 8:1	"Knowledge" puffs up, but love builds up.
1 Corinthians 13:4	Love is patient and kind; love does not envy or boast; it is not arrogant.
1 Corinthians 16:14	Let all that you do be done in love.
2 Corinthians 5:14	For the love of Christ controls us. . . .
Galatians 5:22	But the fruit of the Spirit is love, joy, peace, patience, kindness, goodness, faithfulness. . . .
Ephesians 3:19	To know the love of Christ that surpasses knowledge, that you may be filled with all the fullness of God.
Ephesians 4:2	With all humility and gentleness, with patience, bearing with one another in love.
Ephesians 5:2	And walk in love, as Christ loved us and gave himself up for us. . . .
Colossians 2:2	That their hearts may be encouraged, being knit together in love, to reach all the riches of full assurance of understanding and the knowledge of God's mystery, which is Christ.
1 Timothy 1:5	The aim of our charge is love that issues from a pure heart and a good conscience and a sincere faith.
2 Timothy 1:7	For God gave us a spirit not of fear but of power and love and self-control.
1 Peter 1:8	Though you have not seen him, you love him. Though you do not now see him, you believe in him and rejoice with joy that is inexpressible and filled with glory.

Reference	Content
1 John 3:1	See what kind of love the Father has given to us, that we should be called children of God; and so we are.
1 John 3:16	By this we know love, that he laid down his life for us, and we ought to lay down our lives for the brothers.
1 John 4:7–12	Beloved, let us love one another, for love is from God, and whoever loves has been born of God and knows God. Anyone who does not love does not know God, because God is love. In this the love of God was made manifest among us, that God sent his only Son into the world, so that we might live through him. In this is love, not that we have loved God but that he loved us and sent his Son to be the propitiation for our sins. Beloved, if God so loved us, we also ought to love one another. No one has ever seen God; if we love one another, God abides in us and his love is perfected in us.
1 John 4:18–20	There is no fear in love, but perfect love casts out fear. For fear has to do with punishment, and whoever fears has not been perfected in love. We love because he first loved us. If anyone says, "I love God," and hates his brother, he is a liar; for he who does not love his brother whom he has seen cannot love God whom he has not seen.
1 John 5:3	For this is the love of God, that we keep his commandments. And his commandments are not burdensome.
Jude 1:21	Keep yourselves in the love of God, waiting for the mercy of our Lord Jesus Christ that leads to eternal life.

This is an irresistible love—powerful, gentle, firm to the end. And it calls softly to all God's people, including Muslim women.

THE TRIUNE GOD REACHES OUT

Intercede magazine, November 1995, notes the following: "Any time I have ever told a [Muslim] woman that God really loves her, she just goes to tears," said a female missionary to Turkey. "The personal nature of God is a big jump for her."[4]

Consider Latifa's story, as retold in *Longing to Call Them Sisters*:

> She got hooked and began to read the Bible from cover to cover.
>
> Consistency was what she found, both in Jesus and in Zach and Maria [Christian believers]. "That is rare in my world," she comments. "That started my problem. This guy Jesus was saying things I admired. The teaching was beautiful. But you couldn't have that and throw out the teacher."
>
> Soon her conscience began to nag: "If this is true, you ought to try it."
>
> Every day when she prayed as a Muslim, she would recite the Qur'anic words:
>
> Show me the way.
>
> Don't let me be among those who are lost because of the blindness of their hearts.
>
> One day she gritted her teeth and added, "Okay. Show me. If Jesus Christ is the true way, show me."

The story goes on to describe her experience at a picnic with Zach and Maria.

> Latifa was asked to read aloud the traditional verses from 1 Corinthians 11:
>
> "The Lord Jesus, on the night he was betrayed, took bread, and when he had given thanks, he broke it and said, 'This is my body, which is for you; do this in remembrance of me.' In the same way, after supper he took the cup, saying, 'This cup is the new covenant in my blood; do this, whenever you drink it, in remembrance of me.' For whenever you eat this bread and drink this cup, you proclaim the Lord's death until he comes."

"As I was reading," Latifa recalls, "I was in the Spirit. I was transferred to the upper room. I could see Christ. I could hear Christ. I could sense him saying, 'This is my body, broken for you.'

"I don't know how I looked. Everybody disappeared. Time stopped. I was there with Christ, with the awesome presence of his holiness.

"I started looking at my life with his eyes. Suddenly my life, with which I'd been content, looked terribly dirty. I wanted to run away. Then I heard him say, 'Eat. I came not for you to run away, but on the contrary for you to come close to me.' "

Latifa began to cry, a deep cleansing cry. "Joy replaced everything I felt was wrong," she says. "At that time I knew all my questions about the Trinity had no meaning because I had met Jesus personally."[5]

This joy Latifa felt is the delight of all Bible-believing Christians. Let's see what the Holy Bible teaches about it.

TABLE 10: JOY IN THE HOLY BIBLE

Reference	Content
Psalm 5:11	But let all who take refuge in you rejoice; let them ever sing for joy, and spread your protection over them, that those who love your name may exult in you.
Psalm 16:11	You make known to me the path of life; in your presence there is fullness of joy, at your right hand are pleasures forevermore.
Psalm 21:6	For you make him most blessed forever; you make him glad with the joy of your presence.
Psalm 51:12	Restore to me the joy of your salvation, and uphold me with a willing spirit.
Psalm 71:23	My lips will shout for joy, when I sing praises to you; my soul also, which you have redeemed.
Psalm 105:43	So he brought his people out with joy, his chosen ones with singing.

Reference	Content
Isaiah 12:3	With joy you will draw water from the wells of salvation.
Isaiah 29:19	The meek shall obtain fresh joy in the Lord, and the poor among mankind shall exult in the Holy One of Israel.
Isaiah 35:10	And the ransomed of the Lord shall return and come to Zion with singing; everlasting joy shall be upon their heads; they shall obtain gladness and joy, and sorrow and sighing shall flee away.
Jeremiah 15:16	Your words were found, and I ate them, and your words became to me a joy and the delight of my heart, for I am called by your name, O Lord, God of hosts.
Jeremiah 31:13	Then shall the young women rejoice in the dance, and the young men and the old shall be merry. I will turn their mourning into joy; I will comfort them and give them gladness for sorrow.
Habakkuk 3:18	Yet I will rejoice in the Lord; I will take joy in the God of my salvation.
Acts 13:52	And the disciples were filled with joy and with the Holy Spirit.
Romans 14:17	For the kingdom of God is not a matter of eating and drinking but of righteousness and peace and joy in the Holy Spirit.
Romans 15:13	May the God of hope fill you with all joy and peace in believing, so that by the power of the Holy Spirit you may abound in hope.
Galatians 5:22–23	But the fruit of the Spirit is love, joy, peace, patience, kindness, goodness, faithfulness, gentleness, self-control; against such things there is no law.
Colossians 1:11–12	May you be strengthened with all power, according to his glorious might, for all endurance and patience with joy, giving thanks to the Father, who has qualified you to share in the inheritance of the saints in light.
1 Thessalonians 1:6	And you became imitators of us and of the Lord, for you received the word in much affliction, with the joy of the Holy Spirit.
Hebrews 12:2	Looking to Jesus, the founder and perfecter of our faith, who for the joy that was set before him endured the cross, despising the shame, and is seated at the right hand of the throne of God.

Reference	Content
1 Peter 1:8	Though you have not seen him, you love him. Though you do not now see him, you believe in him and rejoice with joy that is inexpressible and filled with glory.
Jude 1:24	Now to him who is able to keep you from stumbling and to present you blameless before the presence of his glory with great joy.

RESCUED!

Here is another testimony from a Muslim woman who was called to be Christ's own:

> One night Esmat had a dream. Earlier that day, a brother had prayed for her, with beautiful words and kind eyes. "Why can't the mullahs' eyes back home look like that?" she asked herself as she went home. Why couldn't they convey that kind of love: that night she dreamt she was in Iran, going down the street dressed in her chador (head covering). She had to go through a narrow passage lined by rows of armed guards on both sides. They were like walls hemming her in. "I want to be free!" she cried to the Lord. At once the walls fell down, and the face of the man who had prayed for her that day showed through the broken wall.

Later on, she attended a Christian meeting. She recalled:

> A verse flashed into her memory: "Jesus said . . . 'I am the way, the truth, and the life; no one comes to the Father except by me.' "
>
> Esmat fought it. She didn't want to admit that something was changing her. It took her a year to make a decision for Christ. When she found herself following Christ and experiencing his transforming presence, it took some time before she could acknowledge this, even

to herself. She didn't want to be a Christian. But she found that the only peace she experienced came through the church and nowhere else.

When Esmat was a Muslim, God seemed very strict, always watching what she did wrong. When she met God through Christ, he changed from a strict master to a loving, constant Father.[6]

In this testimony, we see another one of the wonderful benefits of knowing Jesus as Savior and Lord—deep and abiding inner peace.

TABLE 11: PEACE IN THE HOLY BIBLE

Reference	Content
Psalm 4:8	In peace I will both lie down and sleep; for you alone, O Lord, make me dwell in safety.
Psalm 37:11	But the meek shall inherit the land and delight themselves in abundant peace.
Psalm 85:10	Steadfast love and faithfulness meet; righteousness and peace kiss each other.
Isaiah 9:6	For to us a child is born, to us a son is given; and the government shall be upon his shoulder, and his name shall be called Wonderful Counselor, Mighty God, Everlasting Father, Prince of Peace.
Isaiah 26:3	You keep him in perfect peace whose mind is stayed on you, because he trusts in you.
Isaiah 32:17	And the effect of righteousness will be peace, and the result of righteousness, quietness and trust forever.
Isaiah 53:5	But he was wounded for our transgressions; he was crushed for our iniquities; upon him was the chastisement that brought us peace, and with his stripes we are healed.
Isaiah 54:10	"For the mountains may depart and the hills be removed, but my steadfast love shall not depart from you, and my covenant of peace shall not be removed," says the Lord, who has compassion on you.

Reference	Content
Ezekiel 37:26	I will make a covenant of peace with them. It shall be an everlasting covenant with them. And I will set them in their land and multiply them, and will set my sanctuary in their midst forevermore.
John 14:27	Peace I leave with you; my peace I give to you. Not as the world gives do I give to you. Let not your hearts be troubled, neither let them be afraid.
Acts 10:36	As for the word that he sent to Israel, preaching good news of peace through Jesus Christ (he is the Lord of all).
Romans 5:1	Therefore, since we have been justified by faith, we have peace with God through our Lord Jesus Christ.
Romans 8:6	To set the mind on the flesh is death, but to set the mind on the Spirit is life and peace.
1 Corinthians 14:33	For God is not a God of confusion but of peace.
Ephesians 2:14–15	For he himself is our peace, who has made us both one and has broken down in his flesh the dividing wall of hostility by abolishing the law of commandments and ordinances, that he might create in himself one new man in place of the two, so making peace.
Philippians 4:7	And the peace of God, which surpasses all understanding, will guard your hearts and your minds in Christ Jesus.
Colossians 1:20	And through him [Jesus] to reconcile to himself all things, whether on earth or in heaven, making peace by the blood of his cross.
Colossians 3:15	And let the peace of Christ rule in your hearts, to which indeed you were called in one body. And be thankful.
1 Thessalonians 5:23	Now may the God of peace himself sanctify you completely, and may your whole spirit and soul and body be kept blameless at the coming of our Lord Jesus Christ.
2 Thessalonians 3:16	Now may the Lord of peace himself give you peace at all times in every way. The Lord be with you all.

CHRIST IS THE "CENTER OF MY LIFE"

Another testimony is provided from the *Church without Walls* outreach letter, dated July–October 2004:

> In 1996 I read a book called *Why I Am Not a Muslim* by Ibn Warraq. The author was a Muslim. He talked about Mohammed, his 23 wives, legal and illegal, his military life, and his teachings. I already knew about Mohammed's behavior, but I continued to justify it. Now, as a Christian, I cannot justify it anymore.
>
> So I started praying to Jesus. My prayers were answered. The first thing I asked Christ was to free me from my cruel Muslim husband. A few days later, my husband left me with three small children. I thanked Christ, and was amazed how quickly and miraculously my prayer was answered. Then I went through a health crisis. I was afraid I would need surgery. I prayed to Christ, and the next test showed that I did not need the surgery. I was convinced that Christ was watching over me.
>
> I was baptized in May of 2000 and had a dream that night. I was bowing to Christ, and He held my right hand. I insisted that He hold my left hand too. He did. Then I got up. My feet were not touching the floor, and I was moving forward without walking, as if I was flying. Then the Holy Spirit came on me as a surprise. It was not just a feeling. I could sense strongly the guidance of the Spirit within me. I had never experienced anything like it in my life. I was amazingly joyful.
>
> Then I started reading the Bible extensively. I studied the book of John very thoroughly. It was obvious that the whole book pointed to Christ's divinity. Then I read the whole Bible from the beginning to the end. Isaiah was very powerful in affirming my belief in Christ's divinity, which I denied before. I have never doubted Christ's deity since then.

Christ has now become the center of my life. My life belongs to Him alone. I cannot repay Him for what He has done for me. He answered all my prayers and forgave my sins.

There are many, many more such testimonies. God in Christ is reaching out to millions of people all across the Muslim world, becoming the center of each humble heart that hears the voice of the Good Shepherd and yields to His call.

BECOMING A BRIDE . . . AGAIN

Christ can become the center of your life, too. Don't let fear or oppression or pride or stubbornness prevent you from experiencing the love, joy, and peace that is yours in Him! Don't let *anything or anyone* keep you from being a part of His bride at the marriage supper of the Lamb, Christ Jesus the Lord!

Let me paint a picture for you here and give it a twist that you may not have thought of before. Christ is coming again to this earth. "Even as you saw Him go, He will come again," the angels said. So imagine that day with me. The heavens are opened and the trumpet sounds and the Son of Man appears on the clouds with power and great glory and with tens of thousands of holy angels shining like the sun. He sends them out to gather His elect from the four winds and raises from the dead those who died in Christ. He gives them new and glorious bodies like His own, and transforms the rest of us in the twinkling of an eye to be fit for glory.

The age-long preparation of the bride of Christ (the church!) is finally complete and He takes her arm, as it were, and leads her to the table. The marriage supper of the Lamb has come. He stands at the head of the table and a great silence falls over the millions of saints. And He says, "This, my beloved, was the meaning of marriage.

This is what it all pointed toward. This is why I created you male and female and ordained the covenant of marriage. Henceforth there will be no more marriage and giving in marriage, for the final reality has come and the shadow can pass away."[7] (See Mark 12:25; Luke 20:34–36)

If you are a Muslim woman and you have read this book with an open heart and mind, we commend your sincere desire to know the truth about women under Islam. Your interest is a result of His intervention on your behalf; He Himself is calling you to listen to His voice. Perhaps someone has given this book to you, or you have unexpectedly found it, or you bought it by "mistake." It doesn't matter. It is in your hands and you have read it—to the end!

We will pray for you, as we pray for each and every woman who comes into contact with this book. Although we do not know you by name, the Lord does. He has known your name from all eternity. We commend you into His care, and trust that He will continue to pursue and chase and woo you—and lavish His love upon you—like a bridegroom longing for His bride.

We encourage you to obtain a copy of the Holy Bible and read it completely. We implore you to seek out Bible-believing Christian women in your communities and get to know them personally.

We ask you to read *The Truth about Islam*,[8] which will guide you to understand the realities of the God of the Holy Bible, Yahweh, His Son Jesus, and His plan of salvation and hope. These realities will lift you up and bring you to a safe place by His heart.

We will pray for the men in your life, that they may be enlightened by your continually sanctified behavior, empowered by the Spirit of Jesus. We will pray that you will be protected from them if you are endangered. We pray that they will be drawn to Jesus by your beautiful new countenance.

If it is your heart's desire to start a new life with Jesus at the center, we offer this prayer to set your feet on His path. If you confess with your mouth and believe in your heart that Jesus Christ is the Way, the Truth, and the Life (see John 14:6), you can be reborn as His very own this very day:

> Dear Lord Jesus, I know that I am a sinner and need your forgiveness. I believe that you died for my sins and that I can come into the presence of God Almighty only through your perfect life and sacrifice, clothed in your righteousness alone. You have called me to be your child, and I ask you to cleanse me and make me your own. Thank you for this free gift of your grace and the promise of life eternal with you. In your Holy Name, Amen.

After praying this prayer wholeheartedly and according to Romans 10:9 ("If you confess with your mouth that Jesus is Lord and believe in your heart that God raised him from the dead, you will be saved"), you are now our sister in God's redemption, and it is your Christian privilege to sing with Mary, the mother of Jesus:

> "My soul magnifies the Lord,
>   and my spirit rejoices in God my Savior,
> for he has looked on the humble estate of his
>   servant.
>   For behold, from now on all generations will call
>   me blessed;
> for he who is mighty has done great things for me,
>   and holy is his name.
> And his mercy is for those who fear him
>   from generation to generation.
> He has shown strength with his arm;
>   he has scattered the proud in the thoughts of their
>   hearts;
> he has brought down the mighty from their thrones
>   and exalted those of humble estate;
> he has filled the hungry with good things,
>   and the rich he has sent empty away.

He has helped his servant Israel,
> in remembrance of his mercy,
as he spoke to our fathers,
> to Abraham and to his offspring forever."
>> Luke 1:46–55

Appendix

These are the very basic tenets of Biblical Christianity, adapted from R.C. Sproul's *Essential Truths of the Christian Faith*.[1]

The Godhead in Biblical Christianity
- Exists as a "complex unity," which is One in essence and three in person: Father, Son, and Holy Spirit.
- All three persons possess all attributes of deity.
- Each person performs specific work and assumes specific responsibilities within the purposes of God.
- Human beings are limited in their ability to comprehend the mystery of the Triune Godhead.
- God is self-existent, omnipotent, omnipresent, omniscient, holy, good, and just.
- God is the father and deliverer of mankind.

The Person of Jesus Christ
- Jesus is the same essence as the Father and is not a created being.
- Jesus is equal to the Father in his divinity, but subordinate to the Father in his role as redeemer.
- His subordination is voluntary and does not put him in an inferior position within the Godhead.

- He was perfectly obedient to the will of God and his righteousness is imputed to those whom he calls to be his own.
- As the only mediator between God and man, Jesus brings about reconciliation between them. This mediation was planned from eternity.
- His role as mediator is superior to that of prophets, priests, and angels.

The Person of the Holy Spirit
- The Holy Spirit possesses all the attributes of divinity and God's full authority.
- The Holy Spirit is not a nebulous "force," but shows personality and enters into relationship with Christians.
- He is to be worshipped and obeyed. He can be offended and grieved.

Creation
- The image and likeness of man is analogous in some way to that of God.
- Human beings are to be stewards of the earth.
- After the Fall, the image of God in mankind has been damaged, as is man's relationship to Him.
- Since the Fall, all men are born with a sinful nature resulting from the original transgression of Adam and Eve.
- Human beings have free will, but since the Fall their wills are in bondage to their sinful natures.
- Only the Holy Spirit can change the human heart and plant within it the desire to know and love God.

Salvation
- Sinful man cannot come into the presence of holy God.
- Man is unable to achieve perfection by his own efforts or good works.
- Man must be saved from ultimate and eternal existence without God through the effort of another on his behalf.

- Jesus Christ, by his perfect life, atoning death, and bodily resurrection, has achieved man's salvation.
- This salvation is completely *of* the Lord and *from* the Lord.
- Christ's atonement satisfies the just wrath of God and allows believers to enter the presence of God clothed in His own perfect garment of righteousness.

Notes

Chapter 1: Creation in the Noble Qur'an

1. Sura 2:34, note 49, "The Arabic may also be translated: 'They bowed down, except Iblis.' In that case Iblis (Satan) would be one of the angels. *But the theory of fallen angels is not usually accepted in Muslim theology.* In Sura 18:50, Iblis is spoken of as a Jinn." Abdullah Yusuf Ali, *The Qur'an: Text, Translation, and Commentary* (Elmhurst: Tahrike Tarsile Qur'an, Inc., U.S. Edition, 2001), 25.

2. Sura 2:30, note 47, "It would seem that the angels, though holy and pure, and endued with power from God [Allah], yet represented only one side of Creation. We may imagine them *without passion or emotion*, of which the highest flower is love. If man was to be endued with emotions, those emotions could lead him to the highest and drag him to the lowest. The power of will or choosing would have to go with them, in order that man might *steer his own bark*. This power of will (when used aright) gave him to some extent a mastery over his own fortunes and over nature, thus bringing him *nearer to the God-like nature*, which has supreme mastery and will. We may suppose the angels had no independent wills of their own: their perfection in other ways reflected God's [Allah's] perfection but could not raise them to the dignity of vicegerency." Ibid., 24.

3. Sura 2:35, note 50, "*Was the Garden of Eden a place on this earth? Obviously not.* For, in verse 36 below, it was after the Fall that the sentence was pronounced: 'On earth will be your dwelling place.' Before the Fall, we must suppose Man to be on another plane altogether—of felicity, innocence, trust, a spiritual existence, with the negation of enmity, want of faith, and all evil." Ibid., 25.

4. Sura 2:36, note 52, " 'Iblis' in 2:34 is apparently the Power of Evil, with the root idea of perversity or enmity. Note the appropriateness of the term on each occasion. Also, 'slipping' from the Garden denotes the idea of *evil gradually tempting man from a higher to a lower state*." Ibid., 25.

5. Sura 2:38, note 56, "Note the transition from the plural 'We' at the beginning of the verse to the singular 'Me' later in the same verse. God [Allah] speaks of Himself usually in the first person plural 'We': it is the plural of respect and honor and is used in human language in Royal proclamations and decrees. But where a *special personal relationship* is expressed the singular 'I' or 'Me' is used, cf. Sura 26:51, etc. In spite of Man's fall, and in consequence of it, assurance of guidance is given. In case man follows the guidance he is free from any fear for the present or the future, and any grief or sorrow for the past. The soul thus freed grows nearer to God [Allah]." Ibid., 26.

6. Anees Zaka and Diane Coleman, *The Truth about Islam* (Phillipsburg, NJ: P&R Publishing), 2004.

7. Sura 20:115, note 2640, ". . . our attention is now called to the prototype of Evil who tempted Adam, the original Man, and to the fact that though man was clearly warned that Evil is his enemy and will only effect his ruin, he *showed so little firmness* that he succumbed to it at once at the first opportunity." Ali, *The Qur'an: Text, Translation, and Commentary*, 814.

8. See Sura 20:120.

9. Sura 7:19, note 1003, "Now the story turns to man. He was placed in a spiritual garden of innocence and bliss, but it was God's [Allah's] Plan to give him a *limited faculty of choice*. All that he was forbidden to do was to *approach* the Tree *of Evil*, but he succumbed to Satan's suggestions." Ibid., 344.

10. Sura 7:20, note 1006, "Our first parents as created by God [Allah] (and this applies to all of us) were innocent in matters material as well as spiritual. They knew no evil. But the faculty of choice, which was given to them and which raised them above the angels, also implied that they had the capacity of evil, which by the *training of their own will,* they were to reject. They were warned of the danger. When they fell, they realized the evil. They were (and we are) still given the chance, in this life on a lower plane, *to make good* and recover the lost status of innocence and bliss." Ibid., 344.

11. Sura 20:118, note 2642, "Not only had the warning been given that Evil is an enemy to man and will effect his destruction, but it was clearly pointed out that all his needs were being met in the Garden of Happiness. Food and *clothing*, drink and shelter, were amply provided for." Ibid., 815.

12. Sura 7:20–22, note 1009, "In the Garden, Satan's deceit stripped off their *raiment of honor* and innocence. In this life on a lower plane he seeks to strip us of the *raiment of righteousness.*" Ibid., 346.

13. Sura 7:26, note 1008, "There is a double philosophy of clothes here, to correspond with the double signification of verse 20 above, as explained in n. 1006. Spiritually, God [Allah] created man 'bare and alone' (6:94): the soul in its naked purity and beauty knew no shame because it knew no guilt: after it was touched by guilt and soiled by evil, its thoughts and deeds became its clothing and adornments, good or bad, honest or meretricious, according to the inner motives which gave them color. So in the case of the body: it is pure and beautiful, as long as it is not defiled by misuse: its clothing and ornaments may be good or meretricious, according to the motives in the mind and character: if good, they are the symbols of purity and beauty: but *the best clothing and ornament we could have comes from righteousness, which covers the nakedness of sin, and adorns us with virtues.*" Ibid., 346.

14. Zaka and Coleman, *The Truth about Islam.*

15. Roland Muller, *Honor and Shame: Unlocking the Door* (USA: Xlibris, 2000).

16. Douglas Jehl, "For Shame: A Special Report: Arab Honor's Price: A Woman's Blood." June 20, 1999. http://polyzine.com/arabwomen.html. Accessed June 26, 2005.

17. Fran Love and Jeleta Eckheart, eds., *Longing to Call Them Sisters: Ministry to Muslim Women* (Pasadena, CA: William Carey Library, 2000), 33–63.

18. Sura 20:123, note 2647, ". . . we have here the consequences of *Guidance* to the individual, viz.: being *saved* from going astray or from *falling into misery* and despair." Ali, *The Qur'an: Text, Translation, and Commentary,* 816.

19. Sura 20:124, note 2648, "The consequences of the rejection of God's [Allah's] guidance are here expressed more individually: *a life narrowed down*, and a blindness that will persist beyond this life. 'A life narrowed down' has many implications: (1) it is a life from which all the beneficent influences of God's [Allah's] wide world are excluded; (2) in looking exclusively to the 'good things' of this life, it misses the true Reality." Ibid., 817.

Chapter 2: Creation and the Fall in the Holy Bible

1. Wayne Grudem, ed., *Biblical Foundations for Manhood and Womanhood* (Wheaton, IL: Crossway, 2002), 77.

2. John Piper, "Manhood and Womanhood: Conflict and Confusion after the Fall" (Desiring God Ministries, May 21, 1989). http://www.desiringgod.org/library/sermons/89/052189.html. Accessed July 5, 2005.

3. John Piper, "Manhood and Womanhood before Sin" (Desiring God Ministries, May 28, 1989). http://www.desiringgod.org/library/sermons/89/052889.html. Accessed July 5, 2005.

4. Dorothy Kelley Patterson, ed., *Woman's Study Bible* (Nashville: Thomas Nelson, 1995).

5. Piper, "Manhood and Womanhood before Sin."

6. Piper, "Manhood and Womanhood: Conflict and Confusion after the Fall."

7. John Piper, "Husbands Who Love like Christ and the Wives Who Submit to Them" (Desiring God Ministries, June 11, 1989). http://www.desiringgod.org/library/sermons/89/061189.html. Accessed June 29, 2005.

8. Piper, "Manhood and Womanhood: Conflict and Confusion after the Fall."

9. Piper, "Manhood and Womanhood before Sin.

10. Kenneth Barker, ed., *NIV Study Bible, New International Version* (Grand Rapids: Zondervan, 1985).

Chapter 3: Men and Women in the Noble Qur'an

1. Anees Zaka and Diane Coleman, *The Truth about Islam* (Phillipsburg, NJ: P&R, 2004).

2. Sura 2:223, note 249, "Sex is not a thing to be ashamed of, or to be treated lightly, or to be indulged to excess. It is as solemn a fact as any in life. It is compared to a husbandman's tilth; it is a serious affair to him: he sows the seed in order to reap the harvest. *But he chooses his own time and mode of cultivation*. He does not sow out of season nor cultivate in a manner which will injure or exhaust the soil. He is wise and considerate and does not run riot."

3. Sura 2:237, note 270, "*Him in whose hands is the marriage tie*: According to Hanafi doctrine this is *the husband himself, who can ordinarily by his act dissolve the marriage.*" Abdullah Yusuf Ali, *The Qur'an: Text, Translation, and Commentary* (Elmhurst: Tahrike Tarsile Qur'an, Inc., U.S. Edition, 2001), 95.

4. Sura 65:1, note 5505, " 'Iddat, as a technical term in divorce law, is explained in Verse note 254 to Sura 2:228. Its general meaning is 'a prescribed period . . .' " Ibid., 1562. Also Sura 2:231, note 261, "If *the man takes back his wife after two divorces*, he must do so only on equitable terms, i.e., he must not put pressure on the woman to prejudice her rights in any way, and they must live

clean and honorable lives, respecting each other's personalities. There are here two conditional clauses: (1) when ye divorce women, and (2) when they fulfill their 'Iddat: followed by two consequential clauses, (3) take them back on equitable terms, or (4) set them free with kindness. The first is connected with the third and the second with the fourth. Therefore *if the husband wishes to resume the marital relations, he need not wait for 'Iddat*. But if he does not so wish, she is free to marry some one else after 'Iddat." Ibid., 91.

5. Sura 4:3, note 508, "Notice the conditional clause about orphans, introducing the rules about marriage. This reminds us of the immediate occasion of the promulgation of this verse. It was after Uhud, when the Muslim community was left with many orphans and widows and some *captives of war*. Their treatment was to be governed by principles of the greatest humanity and equity. The occasion is past, but *the principles remain*. *Marry the orphans* if you are quite sure that you will in that way protect their interests and their property, with perfect justice to them and to your own dependants if you have any. If not, make other arrangements for the orphans." Ibid., 178. Also note 509, "The unrestricted number of wives of the 'Times of Ignorance' was now *strictly limited to a maximum of four*, provided you could treat them with perfect equality, in material things as well as in affection and immaterial things." Ibid., 179.

6. Sura 3:14, note 354, "*The pleasures of this world are first enumerated: women for love; sons for strength and pride*; hoarded riches, which procure all luxuries; the best and finest pedigree horses; cattle, the measure of wealth in the ancient world, as well as the means and symbols of good farming in the modern world; and broad acres of well-tilled land. By analogy, we may include, for our mechanized age, machines of all kinds,—tractors, motorcars, airplanes, the best internal-combustion engines, etc., etc." Ibid., 125.

7. Sura 24:31, note 2984, "The need for modesty is the same in both men and women. But on account of the differentiation of the sexes in nature, temperaments, and social life, a *greater amount of privacy is required for women than for men*, especially in the matter of dress and the uncovering of the bosom." Ibid., 904. Also Sura 24:32, note 2985, " 'Zinat' means both natural beauty and artificial ornaments. I think both are implied here, but chiefly the former. The woman is asked not to make a display of her figure except to the following classes of people: (1) her husband, (2) her near relatives for whom a certain amount of [negligence] is permissible; (3) her women, i.e., her maid-servants, who would be constantly in attendance on her: some Commentators include all believing women; it is not good form in a Muslim household for women to meet other women, except when they are properly dressed; (4) slaves, male

and female, as they would be in constant attendance; but this item would now be blank, with the abolition of slavery; (5) old or infirm men-servants; and (6) infants or small children before they get a sense of sex." Ibid., 904.

8. Sura 24:31, note 2986, "It is *one of the tricks of showy or unchaste women* to tinkle their ankle ornaments, to draw attention to themselves." Ibid., 905.

9. Sura 24:31, note 2987, "While all these details of the purity and good form of domestic life are being brought to our attention, we are clearly reminded that the chief object we should hold in view is our spiritual welfare. *All our brief life on this earth is a probation*, and we must make our individual, domestic, and social life all contribute to our holiness, so that we can get the real success and bliss which is the aim of our spiritual endeavor." Ibid., 905.

10. Sura 33:50, note 3741, ". . . *the Prophet's marriages differed from those of ordinary Muslims*. This is considered under four heads, which we shall examine in the four notes following." Ibid., 1121. Also note 3742, "Head I. Marriage with dower (Sura 4:4): this is the universal Muslim marriage. The difference in the Prophet's case was that there was *no limitation to the number of four (Sura 4:3)*, and women of the People of the Book (Sura 5:6) were not among his wives, but only Believers. These points are not expressly mentioned here, but are inferred by his actual practice." Ibid., 1121.

11. Sura 33:51, note 3749, "In Sura 4:3 it is laid down that more than one wife is not permissible 'if ye fear that ye shall not be able to deal justly with them.' In a Muslim household *there is no room for a 'favorite wife.'* In the special circumstances of the Prophet there were more than one, and he *usually* observed the rule of equality with them, in other things as well as in the rotation of conjugal rights. But considering that his marriages after he was invested with the Prophetic office were mainly dictated by other than conjugal or personal considerations (see note 3706, Sura 33:28), the rotation could not always be observed, though he observed it as much as possible. *This verse absolves him from absolute adherence to a fixed rotation.*" Ibid., 1122.

12. Sura 33:59, note 3764, "This is *for all Muslim women*, those of the Prophet's household, as well as the others. The times were those of insecurity (see next verse) and they were asked to cover themselves with outer garments when walking abroad." Ibid., 1126. Also note 3765, " 'Jilbab,' plural 'Jalabib:' an outer garment; *a long gown covering the whole body*, or a cloak covering the neck and bosom." Ibid. Also note 3766, "The object was not to restrict the liberty of women, but *to protect them from harm and molestation* under the conditions then existing in Medina. In the East and in the West a distinctive public dress of some sort or another has always been a badge of honor or distinction, both among men and women." Ibid.

13. Sura 4:15, note 525, "*Keep them in prison* until some definite order is received. Those who take the crime to be adultery or fornication construe this definite order ('some other way') to mean some definite pronouncement by the Prophet under inspiration; this was the punishment of *flogging* under Sura 24:2." Ibid., 184.

14. Sura 2:228, note 255, "The difference in economic position between the sexes makes the *man's rights and liabilities a little greater than the woman's.*" Ibid., 90.

Chapter 5: Men and Women in Biblical Christianity

1. John Piper, "Jesus, Women, and Men" (Desiring God Ministries, June 4, 1989). http://www.desiringgod.org/library/sermons/89/060489.html. Accessed June 29, 2005.

2. Ibid.

3. John Piper, "Manhood, Womanhood, and the Freedom to Minister" (Desiring God Ministries, June 18, 1989). http://www.desiringgod.org/library/sermons/89/061889.html. Accessed June 29, 2005.

4. John Piper, "Husbands Who Love like Christ and the Wives Who Submit to Them" (Desiring God Ministries, June 11, 1989). http://www.desiringgod.org/library/sermons/89/061189.html. Accessed June 29, 2005.

5. Ibid.

6. "Fifty Crucial Questions." The Council on Biblical Manhood and Womanhood, 2005. http://www.cbmw.com/questions/05.php. Accessed June 29, 2005.

7. John Piper, "Affirming the Goodness of Manhood and Womanhood in All of Life" (Desiring God Ministries, June 25, 1989). http://www.desiringgod.org/library/sermons/89/062589.html. Accessed June 29, 2005.

8. John Piper, "Male and Female He Created Them in the Image of God" (Desiring God Ministries, May 14, 1989). http://www.desiringgod.org/library/sermons/89/051489.html. Accessed June 29, 2005.

Chapter 6: Is Islam the Answer?

1. Leila Ahmed, *Women and Gender in Islam* (New Haven, CT: Yale University Press, 1992), 232, 233.

2. Ibid., 234.

3. Ibid.

4. The following excerpts are from "Lifting the Veil," *Time*, December 3, 2001, 44–59. Emphasis added.

5. http://www.eclipse.co.uk/women/womenasseen.htm. Accessed October 24, 2003.

6. Tim McGirk and Shomali Plain, "Lifting the Veil on Sex Slavery" *Time*, February 18, 2002, 8. Emphasis added.

7. Hammuda Abdul-Ati, Ph.D., "The Status of a Woman in Islam" from "Islam in Focus," http://www.geocities.com/thenewmuslimwoman/StatusofWomeninIslam.html. Accessed June 28, 2005. Emphasis added.

8. Dr. Huwayda Ismaeel. Rendered into English from *Al-Bayaan* magazine, http://www.geocities.com/thenewmuslimwoman/Muslimahs.html. Accessed June 28, 2005. Emphasis added.

9. "Islam and Menses: What You Need to Know." Al-Shahada. http://www.themodernreligion.com/women/w_menses.htm. Accessed June 28, 2005. Emphasis added.

10. "Female Circumcision Ban Nullified," Muslim Women's League. http://www.mwlusa.org/publications/letters/letters.html#egyptviolence. Accessed June 28, 2005. Emphasis added.

11. Siddiqi, Dr. Muzammil H. "Women in mosques—No curtains, no walls, no partitions!" http://www.islamfortoday.com/womeninmosques2.htm. Accessed June 28, 2005. Emphasis added.

12. Yahya M. "Women in Mosques," Islam for Today. http://www.islamfortoday.com/womeninmosques.htm. Accessed June 28, 2005. Emphasis added.

13. Shaukat Omari (book compiler). Online version by M. Ovais Jangda and Hammad Jangda. "Women in Islam," Islam: In the Light of the Final Testament and Traditions. Published by Taurus Publications. http://islamfaqs.tripod.com/ch13.html. Accessed June 28, 2005.

14. Ibid. Emphasis added.

15. "Questions Related to Marriage." Muslim Students' Association at University of Houston. http://www.uh.edu/campus/msa/articles/fatawawom/marriage.html#polygyny. Accessed June 28, 2005. Emphasis added.

16. Omari, "Women in Islam."

17. "Social Interaction in Islam," Muslim Women's League. http://www.mwlusa.org/publications/essays/socialinteraction.html. Accessed June 27, 2005. Emphasis added.

18. "Breaking the Silence," Muslim Women's League. http://www.mwlusa.org/publications/others/breakingsilence.htm. Accessed June 27, 2005.

19. "The Situation of Women in Pakistan," Islam for Today. http://www.islamfortoday.com/pakistanwomen.htm. Accessed June 28, 2005. Emphasis added.

20. Sh. Yusuf Al-Qaradawi, *The Status of Women in Islam.* http://www.jannah.org/sisters/qaradawistatus.html. Accessed June 28, 2005. Emphasis added.

21. "Polygamy." Islam Vision, 2001. http://www.islamvision.org/Polygamy.asp. Accessed June 28, 2005. Emphasis added.

22. "Questions Related to Marriage." Muslim Students' Association at University of Houston. http://www.uh.edu/campus/msa/articles/fatawawom/marriage.html#polygyny. Accessed June 28, 2005. Emphasis added.

23. Ruqaivyah Waris Maqsood, "Islam, Culture and Women," Islam for Today. http://www.islamfortoday.com/ruqaiyyah09.htm. Accessed June 28, 2005. Emphasis added.

24. "An Islamic Perspective on Divorce," Muslim Women's League. http://www.mwlusa.org/publications/positionpapers/divorce.html. Accessed June 28, 2005. Emphasis added.

25. Ruqaivyah Waris Maqsood, "Islam, Culture and Women," Islam for Today. http://www.islamfortoday.com/ruqaiyyah09.htm. Accessed June 28, 2005. Emphasis added.

26. "Women, Marriage, Islamic Dress Etc," Islam for Women. http://islam4women.8m.com/Topics/6.html. Accessed June 28, 2005. Emphasis added.

27. "The Verse of Abuse or the Abused Verse: Al-Qur'an 4:34," Muslim Women's League. From *Dimensions of the Qur'an,* vol. 1, by Sa'dullah Khan. http://www.mwlusa.org/publications/essays/abuseverse.htm. Accessed June 26, 2005. Emphasis added.

28. "Break the Code of Silence. Speak Out Today." Kamilat, 1998. http://kamilat.org/DV/fard.htm#Overview. Accessed June 28, 2005. Emphasis added.

29. Sahar Ali, "Help for Pakistan's acid attack victims." BBC News, August 4, 2003. http://news.bbc.co.uk/1/hi/world/south_asia/3114323.stm. Accessed June 27, 2005. Emphasis added.

30. "Position Paper on Honor Killings," Muslim Women's League, April 1999. http://www.mwlusa.org/publications/positionpapers/hk.html. Accessed June 27, 2005. Emphasis added.

31. In addition, women take second place to male children in Islamic society. In some places, she cannot even go outside unless a male, even if he is only a *child,* accompanies her.

32. Lois Lamya' al Faruqi, "Islamic Traditions and the Feminist Movement: Confrontation or Cooperation?" http://www.jannah.org/sisters/feminism.html. Accessed June 28, 2005. Emphasis added.

33. Hassan al-Turabi, "On the Position of Women in Islam and in Islamic Society," Islam for Today. http://www.islamfortoday.com/turabi01.htm. Accessed June 28, 2005. Emphasis added.

34. Um Amir, "Women and True Education." http://www.themodernreligion.com/women/true-edu.html. Accessed June 27, 2005. Emphasis added.

35. "Questions Related to Marriage," Muslim Students' Association at University of Houston. http://www.uh.edu/campus/msa/articles/fatawawom/marriage.html#polygyny. Accessed June 28, 2005. Emphasis added.

36. Lois Lamya' al-F'aruqi, "Women in a Qur'anic Society." http://www.themodernreligion.com/women/women-society.html. Accessed June 28, 2005. Emphasis added.

37. Harun Yahya, "The Eminence Islam Attaches to Women," Muslim Women's League. http://mwlusa.org/publications/others/eminence_women.htm. Accessed June 27, 2005. Emphasis added.

38. "Issues of Concern for Muslim Women," Muslim Women's League, 1999–2004. http://www.mwlusa.org/publications/positionpapers/issues.html. Accessed June 26, 2005.

39. Jahanara Begum, "The Bitter Lament of a Muslim Woman," Institute for the Secularization of Islamic Society. http://atheism.about.com/gi/dynamic/offsite.htm?site=http%3A%2F%2Fwww.secularislam.org%2Fwomen%2Fbitter.htm. Accessed June 27, 2005.

40. Madeleine Bunting, "Can Islam Liberate Women?" Guardian Unlimited, Dec. 8, 2001. http://www.guardian.co.uk/Archive/Article/0,4273,4314573,00.html. Accessed June 28, 2005. Emphasis added.

41. "The Taliban and Women," Site credits this page as "from the Official Taliban Administration website." http://www.themodernreligion.com/women/taliban.html. Accessed June 28, 2005.

42. "The Verse of Abuse or the Abused Verse: Al-Qur'an 4:34."

43. Ibn Warraq, "Islam's Shame: Lifting the Veil of Tears," from *Why I Am Not a Muslim*. (Amherst, NY: Prometheus Books, 1995). Council for Secular Humanism. http://atheism.about.com/gi/dynamic/offsite.htm?site=http%3A%2F%2Fwww.SecularHumanism.org%2Flibrary%2Ffi%2Fwarraq_17_4.html. Accessed June 27, 2005.

44. Yayha M. "Women's Rights and Equality in Islam," Islam Is for Today. http://www.islamfortoday.com/womensrights2.htm. Accessed June 28, 2005. Emphasis added.

45. Asifa Quraishi, "Opportunities Facing American Muslim Women," Islam Is for Today. http://www.islamfortoday.com/americanmuslimwomenopportunities.htm. Accessed June 28, 2005. Emphasis added.

46. Yahya M. "Muslim Women Reclaim Their Original Rights," Islam Is for Today. http://www.islamfortoday.com/womensrights.htm. Accessed June 28, 2005. Emphasis added.

47. Phil Parshall and Julie Parshall, *Lifting the Veil: The World of Muslim Women* (Waynesboro, GA: Gabriel Publishing, 2002), 13–14.

Chapter 7: A Quest of the Mind and a Cry of the Heart

1. John Piper, "Male and Female He Created Them in the Image of God" (Desiring God Ministries, May 14, 1989). http://www.desiringgod.org/library/sermons/89/051489.html. Accessed June 29, 2005.

2. Muslims believe that He will come again to call all people to the religion of Islam.

3. John Piper, "Jesus Christ, the Bridegroom, Past and Future" (Desiring God Ministries, April 4, 2004). http://www.biblicalpreaching.info/sermonplay.php. Accessed June 29, 2005.

4. Robin Stauffer Skur, "Daughters of Islam." *Intercede*, XI:10, Nov. 1995,

5. Quoted from Alberta Standish and D. Smith, *Muslims and Christians on the Emmaus Road*, by J. Dudley Woodberry, Missions Advanced Research and Communication Center, Monrovia, CA, 1989.

5. Fran Love and Jeleta Eckheart, eds., *Longing to Call Them Sisters: Ministry to Muslim Women* (Pasadena, CA: William Carey Library, 2000), 104–6.

6. Ibid., 111–12.

7. Piper, "Male and Female He Created Them in the Image of God."

8. Anees Zaka and Diane Coleman, *The Truth about Islam* (Phillipsburg, NJ: P&R, 2004).

Appendix

1. R. C. Sproul, *Essential Truths of the Christian Faith* (Wheaton, IL: Tyndale, 1992).

Internet Resources

Abdul-Ati, Hammuda, Ph.D. "The Status of a Woman in Islam" from "Islam in Focus." Accessed at http://www.geocities.com/thenewmuslimwoman/StatusofWomeninIslam.html, June 28, 2005.

Abou-Bakr, Omaima. "Gender Perspectives in Islamic Tradition," Second Annual Minaret of Freedom Institute Dinner, June 26, 1999. Accessed at http://www.minaret.org/gender.htm, June 27, 2005.

Abu Talut. "The Status of Women and Men in Islam," *Islamic Voice*, vol. 14–02, no. 158, February, 2000. Accessed at http://www.islamicvoice.com/february.2000/women.htm#STA, June 26, 2005.

al-F'aruqi, Lois Lamya'. "Islamic Traditions and the Feminist Movement: Confrontation or Cooperation?" Accessed at http://www.jannah.org/sisters/feminism.html, June 28, 2005.

al-F'aruqi, Lois Lamya'. "Women in a Qur'anic Society." Accessed at http://www.themodernreligion.com/women/women-society.html, June 28, 2005.

Ali, Sahar. "Help for Pakistan's Acid Attack Victims," BBC News, August 4, 2003. Accessed at http://news.bbc.co.uk/1/hi/world/south_asia/3114323.stm, June 27, 2005.

Al-Qaradawi, Sh. Yusuf. "The Status of Women in Islam," Jannah. org. Accessed at http://www.jannah.org/sisters/qaradawistatus.html, June 28, 2005.

Al-Qaradawi, Yousuf. "Qaradawi on Free-Mixing of Men and Women." Accessed at http://www.themodernreligion.com/women/free-mixing-qaradawi.html, June 26, 2005.

al-Turabi, Hassan. "On the Position of Women in Islam and in Islamic Society," Islam for Today. Accessed at http://www.islamfortoday.com/turabi01.htm, June 28, 2005.

Amanullah, Shahed. "Indian Muslims Consider a Divorce From 'Triple Talaq,' " Halalfire Media, 2001–2005. Accessed at http://www.altmuslim.com/news_comments.php?id=1252_0_26_0_C, June 26, 2005.

Ambah, Faiza Saleh. "Saudi Women Talk Rights," iviews.com, from the *Christian Science Monitor*. Accessed at http://www.iviews.com/Articles/articles.asp?ref=CH0407-2381, June 26, 2005.

Badawi, Jamal A. "The Status of Women in Islam." Accessed at http://www.iad.org/books/S-women.html, June 28, 2005.

Badran, Margot. "Islamic Feminism: What's in a Name?" *Al-Ahram Weekly Online*, 17–23 January, 2002. Accessed at http://weekly.ahram.org.eg/2002/569/cu1.htm, June 26, 2005.

Bardach, Ann Louise. "In the Name of Islam—Women Are Being Abused, Even Mutilated," from *Reader's Digest*, March 1994. Accessed at http://www.themodernreligion.com/ugly/ugly_women.htm, June 26, 2005.

Begum, Jahanara. "The Bitter Lament of a Muslim Woman," Institute for the Secularization of Islamic Society. Accessed at http://atheism.about.com/gi/dynamic/offsite.htm?site=http%3A%2F%2Fwww.secularislam.org%2Fwomen%2Fbitter.htm, June 27, 2005.

Beiruty, Hikmat. "Muslim Women in Sport," *Nida'ul Islam Magazine*, July/August 1997. Accessed at http://www.islam.org.au/articles/19/women.htm, June 26, 2005.

bint Ellison, Naasira. "Women: the Distorted Image of Muslim Women," thetruereligion.org, March 30, 2004. Accessed at http://thetruereligion.org/modules/wfsection/article.php?articleid=39, June 26, 2005.

Bunting, Madeleine. "Can Islam Liberate Women?" Guardian Unlimited, Dec. 8, 2001. Accessed at http://www.guardian.co.uk/Archive/Article/0,4273,4314573,00.html, June 28, 2005.

Carlo, Shariffa. "The Muslim Woman." Accessed at http://www.themuslimwoman.com/themuslimwoman.htm, June 26, 2005.

Carpenter, Mackenzie. "Muslim Women Say Veil Is More about Expression Than Oppression," Post-Gazette.com, Oct. 28, 2001, PG Publishing. Accessed at http://www.post-gazette.com/headlines/20011028muslimwomennat3p3.asp, June 26, 2005.

Carvello, Waheeda. "The Impact of Marginalizing Women in the Islamic Movement," beliefnet, Crescent International, 2000. Accessed at http://www.beliefnet.com/story/47/story_4763_1.html, June 27, 2005.

Dagher, Hamdun. *The Position of Women in Islam* (Villach: Austria: Light of Life). Accessed at www.light-of-life.com/eng/reveal/, June 26, 2005. See chapters 1, 4, 9, 12, 15, 18, 21, 25–26.

El-Monjjid, Sh. Mohammad Saleh. "The Merits of Islaam." Accessed at http://ssmu.mcgill.ca/icn/merits.html, June 28, 2005.

Emerick, Yahiya and Reshma Baig. "The War of the Women." Accessed at http://www.themodernreligion.com/women/w_war.htm, June 26, 2005.

Fadl, Mona Abul. "Understanding Gender in Muslim Societies," Muslim Women Studies. Accessed at http://www.muslimwomenstudies.com/GENDER1.htm, June 28, 2005.

Gattas, Kim. "Beirut Hosts 'Honour Killing' Conference," BBC News, May 13, 2001. Accessed at http://news.bbc.co.uk/1/hi/world/middle_east/1328238.stm, June 26, 2005.

Georgi, Lydia. "Saudi's Human Rights Watchdog Getting Ready to Go," Middle East Online, March 5, 2004. Accessed at http://www.middle-east-online.com/english/?id=9143, June 26, 2005.

Halsall, Paul. "Jewish History Sourcebook: Islam and the Jews: the Status of Jews and Christians in Muslim Lands, 1772 CE," Internet Jewish History Sourcebook, July, 1998. Accessed at http://www.fordham.edu/halsall/jewish/1772-jewsinislam.html, June 26, 2005.

Hamed, Sheikh Mohammad Abdelhaleem. "How to Make Your Husband Happy," The Modern Religion. Accessed at http://www.themodernreligion.com/women/happyhubby.html, June 26, 2005.

Haroon, Fariha Razak. "Women Are Falling Behind in Pakistan," The Modern Religion. Accessed at http://www.themodernreligion.com/women/w_pak.htm, June 26, 2005.

Haydar, Maysan. "Veiled? One Muslim Woman on Her Choice to Veil." Accessed at http://admin.muslimsonline.com/~huma/sisters/veiled.html, June 26, 2005.

Hendricks, Shaykh Seraj. "Authority and the Abuse of Power in Muslim Marriages," Women's Conference of the Second International Islamic Unity Conference, Washington, D.C., August 8, 1998, The Modern Religion. Accessed at http://www.themodernreligion.com/women/abuse-marriage.html, June 26, 2005.

Hymowitz, Kay S. "Liberation's Limits," WSJ.com Opinion Journal, March 8, 2003. Accessed at http://www.opinionjournal.com/extra/?id=110003173, July 10, 2004.

Ismaeel, Dr. Huwayda. Rendered into English from *Al-Bayaan Magazine*. Accessed at http://www.geocities.com/thenewmuslimwoman/Muslimahs.html, June 28, 2005.

Jabbaar, Salman Hassan. "The Place of Women in Christianity and Islam," 1994. Accessed at http://www.answering-islam.org/women/place.html, June 27, 2005.

Jehl, Douglas. "For Shame: A Special Report: Arab Honor's Price: A Woman's Blood," June 20, 1999. Accessed at http://polyzine.com/arabwomen.html, June 26, 2005.

Kim, Lucian. "Tenacity under Afghan Burqas," csmonitor.com, the *Christian Science Monitor*, July 19, 2000. Accessed at http://www.csmonitor.com/atcsmonitor/specials/women/rights/rights071900.html, June 26, 2005.

Mann, Judy. "Focusing on the Tragedy of Afghan Women," Islam for Today. From the *Washington Post*, October 30, 1998. Accessed at http://www.islamfortoday.com/afghanistanwomen6.htm, July 11, 2004.

Maqsood, Ruqaiyyah Waris. "Are There More Women Than Men in Hell?" The Modern Religion. Accessed at http://www.themodernreligion.com/women/w-hell.html, June 26, 2005.

Maqsood, Ruqaiyyah Waris. "Islam, Culture and Women." Islam for Today. Accessed at http://www.islamfortoday.com/ruqaiyyah09.htm, June 28, 2005.

Morris, Jennifer. "The Changing Face of Women in Bangladesh." Accessed at http://www.columbia.edu/cu/sipa/PUBS/SLANT/SPRING97/morris.html, June 26, 2005.

Naik, Zakir. "Polygamy—Definition and Guidelines," The Modern Religion. Accessed at http://www.themodernreligion.com/women/w_poly-znaik.html, June 26, 2005.

Nutt, Samantha. "Freedom Denied," Macleans.ca, Rogers Media Inc., July 1, 2003. Accessed at http://www.macleans.ca/topstories/

world/article.jsp?content=20030701_61916_61916, July 11, 2004.

Philips, Abu Ameenah Bilal. "Islam's Position on Polygamy," BilalPhilips.com, 2000–2001. Accessed at http://www.bilalphilips.com/abouthim/artic04a.htm, June 27, 2005.

Phillips, Rebecca. "Islam through the Front Door," beliefnet. Interview with Asra Nomani, founder of the Muslim Women's Freedom Tour. Accessed at http://www.beliefnet.com/story/168/story_16827_1.html?rnd=59, June 27, 2005.

Piper, John. "Affirming the Goodness of Manhood and Womanhood in All of Life," Desiring God Ministries, June 25, 1989. Accessed at http://www.desiringgod.org/library/sermons/89/062589.html, June 29, 2005.

Piper, John. "Husbands Who Love Like Christ and the Wives Who Submit to Them," Desiring God Ministries, June 11, 1989. Accessed at http://www.desiringgod.org/library/sermons/89/061189.html, June 29, 2005.

Piper, John. "Jesus, Women, and Men," Desiring God Ministries, June 4, 1989, Accessed at http://www.desiringgod.org/library/sermons/89/060489.html, June 29, 2005.

Piper, John. "Male and Female He Created Them in the Image of God," Desiring God Ministries, May 14, 1989. Accessed at http://www.desiringgod.org/library/sermons/89/051489.html, June 29, 2005.

Piper, John. "Manhood and Womanhood before Sin," Desiring God Ministries, May 28, 1989. Accessed at http://www.desiringgod.org/library/sermons/89/052889.html, July 5, 2005.

Piper, John. "Manhood and Womanhood: Conflict and Confusion after the Fall," Desiring God Ministries, May 21, 1989. Accessed at http://www.desiringgod.org/library/sermons/89/052189.html, July 5, 2005.

Piper, John. "Manhood, Womanhood, and the Freedom to Minister," Desiring God Ministries, June 18, 1989. Accessed at http://www.desiringgod.org/library/sermons/89/061889.html, June 29, 2005.

Prusher, Ilene R. "Kuwaiti Women Seek Right to Vote," csmonitor.com, the *Christian Science Monitor*, August 8, 2000. Accessed at http://www.csmonitor.com/atcsmonitor/specials/women/rights/rights080800.html, June 26, 2005.

Prusher, Ilene R. "Two Homes, Two Families, Two Wives," csmonitor.com, the *Christian Science Monitor*, August 10, 2000. Accessed at http://www.csmonitor.com/atcsmonitor/specials/women/rights/rights081000.html, June 26, 2005.

Prusher, Ilene R. "Symbol of Both Oppression and Freedom," csmonitor.com, the *Christian Science Monitor*, August 11, 2000. Accessed at http://www.csmonitor.com/atcsmonitor/specials/women/rights/rights081100.html, June 26, 2005.

Prusher, Ilene R. "Small Steps, but the Pace Quickens," csmonitor.com, the *Christian Science Monitor*, August 7, 2000. Accessed at http://www.csmonitor.com/atcsmonitor/specials/women/rights/rights080700.html, June 26, 2005.

Qazi, Abdullah. "The Plight of the Afghan Women," Afghanistan Online. Accessed at http://www.afghan-web.com/woman/, June 26, 2005.

Quraishi, Asifa. "Opportunities Facing American Muslim Women," Islam for Today. Accessed at http://www.islamfortoday.com/americanmuslimwomenopportunities.htm, June 28, 2005.

Rafiqul-Haqq, M., Newton, P. "The Place of Women in Pure Islam," 1996. Accessed at http://debate.domini.org/newton/womeng.html, January 1, 2004.

Ragab, Noha. "The Record Set Straight: Women in Islam Have Rights." Accessed at http://www.jannah.org/sisters/noha.html, June 27, 2005.

Rauf, Imam Feisal Abdul. "Women and Islam," pbs.org, WGBH Educational Foundation, 1995–2005. Accessed at http://www.pbs.org/wgbh/pages/frontline/shows/muslims/themes/women.html, June 27, 2005.

Shahid, Aisha Atiq. "The Muslim Lady: Her Role and Her Honor." Accessed at http://www.geocities.com/~abdulwahid/women.html, June 26, 2005.

Shibli. "In Defence of the Taliban," The Modern Religion. Accessed at http://www.themodernreligion.com/women/w_afghan-reply.htm, June 26, 2005.

Siddiqi, Dr. Muzammil H. "Women in Mosques—No Curtains, No Walls, No Partitions!" Islam for Today. Accessed at http://www.islamfortoday.com/womeninmosques2.htm, June 28, 2005.

UmAmir. "Women and True Education," The Modern Religion. Accessed at http://www.themodernreligion.com/women/true-edu.html, June 27, 2005.

Walter, Natasha. "Where Are the Women?" Guardian Unlimited, April 25, 2003. Accessed at http://www.guardian.co.uk/Iraq/Story/0,2763,943256,00.html, June 26, 2005.

Watanabe, Teresa. "Breaching the Wall at Prayer," *Los Angeles Times*, 2005. Accessed at http://www.latimes.com/news/local/la-me-muswomen27jun27,0,2991977,print.story?coll=la-home-headlines, June 27, 2005.

Warraq, Ibn. "Islam's Shame: Lifting the Veil of Tears," from *Why I Am Not a Muslim*. (Amherst, NY: Prometheus Books, 1995). Council for Secular Humanism. Accessed at http://atheism.about.com/gi/dynamic/offsite.htm?site=http%3A%2F%2Fwww.SecularHumanism.org%2Flibrary%2Ffi%2Fwarraq_17_4.html, June 27, 2005.

Yahya, Harun. "The Eminence Islam Attaches to Women," Muslim Women's League. Accessed at http://www.mwlusa.org/publications/others/eminence_women.htm, June 27, 2005.

Yahya, M. "Muslim Women Reclaim Their Original Rights," Islam for Today. Accessed at http://www.islamfortoday.com/womensrights.htm, June 28, 2005.

Yahya, M. "Women in Mosques," Islam for Today. Accessed at http://www.islamfortoday.com/womeninmosques.htm, June 27, 2005.

Yayha, M. "Women's Rights and Equality in Islam," Islam for Today. Accessed at http://www.islamfortoday.com/womensrights2.htm, June 28, 2005.

Young, Harry. "But I Love Him . . ." Answering Islam. Accessed at http://www.answering-islam.org/Marriage/lovehim.html, June 27, 2005.

ONLINE RESOURCES AND ARTICLES BY TITLE (NO AUTHOR LISTED)

"1999 report: The Taliban's War on Women—A Health and Human Rights Crisis in Afghanistan." Physicians for Human Rights. Accessed at www.phrusa.org/research/health_effects/exec.html, June 26, 2005.

"Afghanistan: Taliban's War on Women." Physicians for Human Rights Newsletter, October 1998. Accessed at http://www.thirdworldtraveler.com/Life_Death_ThirdWorld/Taliban_WarWomen.html, June 26, 2005.

"An Islamic Perspective on Divorce." Muslim Women's League. Accessed at http://www.mwlusa.org/publications/positionpapers/divorce.html, June 27, 2005.

"An Islamic Perspective on Women's Dress." Muslim Women's League. Accessed at http://www.mwlusa.org/publications/positionpapers/hijab.html, June 27, 2005.

"Ask about Islam." Islam Online, 1999–2005. Accessed at http://www.islamonline.net/askaboutislam/display.asp?hquestionID=5718, June 26, 2005.

"Break the Code of Silence. Speak Out Today." Kamilat, 1998. Accessed at http://kamilat.org/DV/fard.htm#Overview, June 28, 2005.

"Breaking the Silence." Muslim Women's League. Accessed at http://www.mwlusa.org/publications/others/breakingsilence.htm, June 27, 2005.

"Chapter 13: Women in Islam." Accessed at http://islamfaqs.tripod.com/ch13.html, June 28, 2005.

"Female Circumcision Ban Nullified." Muslim Women's League. Accessed at http://www.mwlusa.org/publications/letters/letters.html#egyptviolence, June 27, 2005.

"Female Genital Mutilation (FGM) in Africa, The Middle East and Far East." Accessed at http://www.religioustolerance.org/fem_cirm.htm, June 26, 2005.

"Fifty Crucial Questions." The Council on Biblical Manhood and Womanhood, 2005. Accessed at http://www.cbmw.com/questions/05.php, June 29, 2005.

"Hadith of Bukhari." Accessed at http://www.sacred-texts.com/isl/bukhari/index.htm.

"The Holy Bible, English Standard Version." Accessed at http://www.gnpcb.org/esv/.

"International Community Should Pay More Than Lip Service to Plight of Afghan Women." Amnesty International, February 6, 1998. Accessed at http://web.amnesty.org/library/Index/engASA110011998, June 27, 2995.

Interview with Amina Wadud. PBS online and wgbh/frontline, 2002. Accessed at http://www.pbs.org/wgbh/pages/frontline/shows/muslims/interviews/wadud.html, June 26, 2005.

"Islam: A Primer." Ethics and Public Policy Center, September 8, 2002. Accessed at http://www.eppc.org/publications/pubID.1536/pub_detail.asp, July 10, 2004.

"Islam and Menses: What You Need to Know." Al-Shahada. Accessed at http://www.themodernreligion.com/women/w_menses.htm, June 28, 2005.

"Issues of Concern for Muslim Women." Muslim Women's League, 1999–2004. Accessed at http://www.mwlusa.org/publications/positionpapers/issues.html, June 26, 2005.

"Misconceptions about Women in Islam." Accessed at http://www.sistersinislam.net/modules.php?op=modload&name=Sections&file=index&req=viewarticle&artid=14, June 28, 2005.

MSA-USC Hadith Database. Accessed at http://www.usc.edu/dept/MSA/reference/searchhadith.html, June 26, 2005.

"Muslim Women Reclaim Their Original Rights." Accessed at http://www.members.aol.com/yahyam/mwomen.html, June 26, 2005.

"Pakistan Rape Victim Must Get Justice—President." Reuters, 2005. Accessed at http://www.reuters.com/newsArticle.jhtml?type=worldNews&storyID=8925669, June 29, 2005.

"Polygamy." Islam Vision, 2001. Accessed at http://www.islamvision.org/Polygamy.asp, June 26, 2005.

"Position Paper on 'Honor Killings.'" Muslim Women's League. Accessed at http://www.mwlusa.org/publications/positionpapers/hk.html, June 27, 2005.

"Purdah." Islam Vision, 2001. Accessed at http://www.islamvision.org/Purdah.asp, June 26, 2005.

"Questions Related to Marriage." Muslim Students' Association at University of Houston. Accessed at http://www.uh.edu/campus/msa/articles/fatawawom/marriage.html#polygyny, June 28, 2005.

"Quran Translation: Abdullah Yusuf Ali." Accessed at http://emuslim.com/QuranYa.asp.

"Results of Kamilat's Community Development Survey." Kamilat, 1999. Accessed at http://kamilat.org/Surveys/survey1.htm, June 26, 2005.

"Results of Kamilat's Community Development Survey on Arranged Marriages." Kamilat, 1999. Accessed at http://kamilat.org/Surveys/survey2.htm, June 26, 2005.

"Results of Kamilat's Community Development Survey on Contemporary Roles of Muslim Women." Kamilat, 1999. Accessed at http://kamilat.org/Surveys/survey3.htm, June 26, 2005.

"The Situation of Women in Pakistan." Islam for Today. Accessed at http://www.islamfortoday.com/pakistanwomen.htm, June 28, 2005.

"Social Interaction in Islam." Muslim Women's League. Accessed at http://www.mwlusa.org/publications/essays/socialinteraction.html, June 27, 2005.

"Talaq." Islam Vision, 2001. Accessed at http://www.islamvision.org/Talaq.asp, June 26, 2005.

"The Taliban." Accessed at http://www.webster.edu/~woolflm/taliban.html, June 28, 2005.

"The Taliban and Women." From the Official Taliban Administration website. Accessed at http://www.themodernreligion.com/women/taliban.html, June 28, 2005.

"The Treatment of Women in Islam." Arabic Outreach Bible Ministry, 1998–2001. Accessed at http://www.arabicbible.com/christian/Women_in_Islam.htm, June 26, 2005.

"UNICEF Executive Director targets violence against women." Accessed at http://www.unicef.org/newsline/00pr17.htm, June 26, 2005.

"The Verse of Abuse or the Abused Verse: Al-Qur'an 4:34." Muslim Women's League. Accessed at http://www.mwlusa.org/publications/essays/abuseverse.htm, June 26, 2005.

"Women and Islam." Accessed at http://notendur.centrum.is/~snorrigb/hijab.htm, June 26, 2005.

"Women, Marriage, Islamic Dress, Etc." Accessed at http://islam4women.8m.com/Topics/6.html, June 28, 2005.

"Women's Rights." Islam Vision, 2001. Accessed at http://www.islamvision.org/WomensRights.asp, June 26, 2005.

"Women's Rights and Equality in Islam." Accessed at http://members.aol.com/yahyam/equality.html, June 26, 2005.

"Words to My Muslim Sister." "The Muslim Creed," vol. 3, no. 2, February 1995. The Dear of Islamic Heritage. Accessed at http://www.usc.edu/dept/MSA/humanrelations/womeninislam/advicetowomen.html, June 26, 2005.

GENERAL WEBSITES

These are homepages and articles about Islam, women in Islam, and Christianity and Islam.

http://www.islamicity.com/

http://www.usc.edu/dept/MSA/humanrelations/womeninislam/

http://www.columbia.edu/cu/lweb/indiv/mideast/cuvlm/women.html

http://www.altmuslim.com/

http://www.themodernreligion.com

http://www.themodernreligion.com/women/w_dv.htm

http://www.faithfreedom.org/

http://www.salaam.co.uk/news/index.php

http://www.messageonline.org/

http://www.themuslimwoman.com/

http://www.muslimwomenstudies.com/

http://www.skidmore.edu/academics/arthistory/ah369/finalveil.htm (a comprehensive discussion of veiling plus a bibliography on related topics)

http://admin.muslimsonline.com/~huma/sisters/

http://www.islamonline.net/English/index.shtml

http://www.uga.edu/islam/Islamwomen.html

http://us.geocities.com/rfaizer/biblio/islam_inst_5.html

http://www.infidels.org/library/modern/theism/islam/index.shtml

http://www.danielpipes.org/

http://www.islam-in-focus.com/

http://www.understanding-islam.com/
    http://www.understanding-islam.com/related/search.asp?searchstr=women&lookin=1&image1.x=11&image1.y=11

http://www.islamvision.org/index.asp

http://www.iran-e-azad.org/english/book_on_women.html

http://www.beliefnet.com/search/search_site_results.asp?search_for=Islam&to_search=whole_site

http://meria.idc.ac.il/

http://kamilat.org/

http://www.mwlusa.org/welcome.html

http://www.islam-christianity.com/

http://www.islamreview.com/

http://answering-islam.org/Women/inislam.html

http://www.answering-islam.org/Responses/Azeem/index.htm
http://www.answering-islam.org/Testimonies/cati.html

http://www.submission.org/women/
http://www.submission.org/polygamy.html
http://www.submission.org/women/wives.html
http://www.submission.org/women/marriage.html
http://www.submission.org/women/divorce.html
http://www.submission.org/women/Aisha.html
http://www.submission.org/dress.html

www.islamfortoday.com
http://www.islamfortoday.com/women.htm#Rights

http://www.domini.org/lam/real_life_experiences.html
http://www.domini.org/lam/Marianne.html
http://www.domini.org/lam/warnings.html
http://www.domini.org/lam/jan.html
http://www.domini.org/lam/nadia.html
http://www.domini.org/lam/gypsy.html
http://www.domini.org/lam/tina.html

http://members.tripod.com/safia71/men_in_islam.htm

http://members.tripod.com/safia71/women_in_islam.htm

http://islam4women.8m.com

www.jannah.org/sisters/
http://www.jannah.org/sisters/women.html

http://womenshistory.about.com/od/islamandwomen/

http://www.aljazeerah.info/Islam/Islam.htm

http://www.ummah.net/

http://www.iran-e-azad.org/english

http://atheism.about.com/od/womeninislam/

http://atheism.about.com/gi/dynamic/offsite.htm?site=http%3A%2F%2Fanswering-islam.org%2FBehindVeil%2Fbtv3.html%23CH3

http://www.apostatesofislam.com/main.htm

http://www.rawa.org/

Index of Biblical Texts

Genesis
1:26—17
1:26-28—15-16
1:27—20
2:7—20
2:7-25—16-17
2:8-15—5
2:15—20
2:15-17—20, 21
2:18—20
2:20—20
2:23—19, 20
3:1-7—19, 21-22
3:3—23
3:8—11
3:8-13—25
3:9—20
3:11—20
3:14-15—26
3:16—27, 28, 29, 30
3:17—28
3:17-19—30-31
3:20—20
3:20-24—32
4:7—28, 29
24:67—59
49:9—29

Exodus
20:5—59
20:17—60
34:14—59

Deuteronomy
4:24—59
5:9—59
6:15—59
17:17—60, 61
24:5—60

Joshua
24:19—59

1 Samuel
1:8—60
25—31
25:23-35—80

Esther—31

Job
28:18—24

Psalms
4:8—111
5:11—108
16:11—108
21:6—108
37:11—111
51:6—24
51:12—108
71:23—108
85:10—111
86:8—18
103:20—4
105:43—108
111:10—24
148:2—4

Proverbs
1:2—24
5:18—60
8:11—24
9:10—24
18:22—60
19:14—60
31:10-31—61-63

Song of Songs
7:10—60

Isaiah
9:6—111
12:3—109
14:12-15—3
26:3—111
29:19—100
32:17—111
35:10—109
46:9—18
53:5—111
54:5—60
54:10—111
64:6—10

151

Jeremiah
15:16—109
31:13—109
31:32—60

Ezekiel
37:26—112

Hosea
2:16—61

Habakkuk
3:18—109

Malachi
2:15—61

Matthew
5:5—69
5:27—63
5:28—67
5:31-32—63-64
9:22—64
13:43—69
15:28—64
19:3-8—73
25:41—3
26:10—64
27:19—31
27:55—64

Mark
7:26—64
12:25—115

Luke
1:46-55—116-17
2:13-15—4
2:51—64
7:37-38—64-65
7:47-48—65
8:2—65
10:38—65
10:39—65
10:42—65
11—68
11:27-28—65
13:10-17—68
13:12—65
15:10—4
20:34-36—115
23:55—65
24:10—65

John
4:7—66
8:10-11—66
14:6—116
14:27—112
15:13—104
17:26—105
19:25—66
19:26—66
20:16—66
20:18—66

Acts
2:18—69
5:14—69
8:3—70
8:12—70
9:2—70
10:36—112
13:52—109
16:14—70
17:12—70
17:34—70
18:26—70
22:4—70

Romans
3:21-26—32
5:1—112
5:5—105
5:8—105
8:6—112
8:39—105
10:9—116
13:8—105

14:17—109
15:13—109
16:12—70

1 Corinthians
7—80
7:2-4—73
7:10-11—74
7:14—74
7:28—74
7:34—74
8:1—105
11—107
11:3—74
11:12—74
13:4—105
14:33—112
14:33-35—71
14:35—74
16:14—105

2 Corinthians
5:14—105
11:2—74

Galatians
5:22—105
5:22-23—109

Ephesians
2:14-15—112
3:19—105
4:2—105
5:2—105
5:21—78
5:21-33—76

Philippians
3:9—32
4:7—112

Colossians
1:11-12—109
1:20—112

2:2—105
3:15—112
3:18-19—74

1 Thessalonians
1:6—109
5:23—112

2 Thessalonians
3:16—112

1 Timothy
1:5—105
2:8-12—71
3:1-5—75

2 Timothy
1:7—105

Titus
1:6-9—75
2:3-5—75

Hebrews
12:2—109

James
1:5—24

1 Peter
1:8—110

1:12—4
3:1—78
3:1-7—76

1 John
3:1—106
3:16—106
4:7-12—106
4:18-20—106
5:3—106

Jude
1:6—3
1:9—4
1:21—106
1:24—110

Index of Qur'anic Texts

Sura
2:29-39—1
2:30—1-2, 123n.2
2:30-39—1
2:31—2
2:32—2
2:33—2
2:34—2, 123n.1, 124n.4
2:35—2, 123n.3
2:36—2, 123n.3, 124n.4
2:37—2
2:38—3, 124n.5
2:39—3
2:221—36
2:222—36
2:223—126n.2
2:228—41, 126n.4, 129n.14
2:231—36, 126n.4
2:236—36
2:237—126n.3
2:241—36
3:14—41, 127n.6

4:3—36, 127n.5, 128n.10, 128n.11
4:4—36, 128n.10
4:15—41, 129n.13
4:19—36
4:20—36
4:34—36, 80
4:43—41
4:128—37
4:129—37
5:6—128n.10
6:94—125n.13
7:19—7, 124n.9
7:19-27—7-8
7:20—7, 124n.10
7:20-22—125n.12
7:21—7
7:22—7
7:23—7
7:24—7
7:25—7
7:26—8, 9, 125n.13
7:27—8
18:50—123n.1
20:115—6, 124n.7
20:115-124—6-7

20:116—6
20:117—6
20:118—6, 124n.11
20:119—6
20:120—6, 124n.8
20:121—6
20:122—6
20:123—6, 125n.18
20:124—7, 125n.19
24:2—132
24:31—42, 127n.7, 128n.8, 128n.9
24:32—37, 127n.7
24:60—42
26:51—124n.5
33:28—128n.11
33:33—42
33:50—37, 128n.10
33:51—37, 128n.11
33:52—37
33:59—42, 48, 128n.12
60:10—37
65:1—37, 126n.4
65:4—37
65:6—38

Anees Zaka (B.A., M.Div., a Middle Eastern university and seminary; Th.M., D.Min., Westminster Theological Seminary, Philadelphia; Ph.D., Ed.D, American University of Biblical Studies, Atlanta) is the founder and director of Church Without Walls (Presbyterian Church in America) and founder and president of Biblical Institute for Islamic Studies. Not only has Dr. Zaka completed many years of study and research on the subject of Islam, he has also given a lifetime of service in ministry to Muslims both overseas and in North America. Dr. Zaka is co-author of *Muslims and Christians at the Table: Promoting Biblical Understanding among North American Muslims,* with Bruce A. McDowell, and *The Truth about Islam: The Noble Qur'an's Teachings in Light of the Holy Bible,* with Diane Coleman.

Diane Coleman (B.S., Pennsylvania State University) has served as a speech and language therapist, a program director for the profoundly handicapped, a biochemical research technician, and a curriculum coordinator and educator. As an educator, she and her family also spent several months overseas living in a predominantly Islamic country. Mrs. Coleman's published writings include *The Truth About Islam: The Noble Qur'an's Teachings in Light of the Holy Bible,* with Anees Zaka, a literary guide to the classic *Robin Hood,* two teaching manuals on phonics, and a privately commissioned company history entitled *It All Began with a Number Two Lead Pencil.*